GREEN
GUIDE
FOR ARTISTS

QUARRY

GREEN GUIDE
FOR ARTISTS

KAREN MICHEL
GALLERY PROFILES BY KRISTEN HAMPSHIRE

NONTOXIC RECIPES, GREEN ART IDEAS, & RESOURCES FOR THE ECO-CONSCIOUS ARTIST

BEVERLY MASSACHUSETTS

QUARRY BOOKS

First published in the United States of America by
Quarry Books, a member of
Quayside Publishing Group
100 Cummings Center
Suite 406-L
Beverly, Massachusetts 01915-6101
Telephone: (978) 282-9590
Fax: (978) 283-2742
www.quarrybooks.com

Library of Congress Cataloging-in-Publication Data
Michel, Karen.
  Green guide for artists : nontoxic recipes, green art ideas, and resources for the eco-conscious artist /
Karen Michel.
    p. cm.
  ISBN-13: 978-1-59253-518-7
  ISBN-10: 1-59253-518-6
  1. Artists' materials. 2. Art—Environmental aspects. I. Title.
  N8530.M53 2009
  702.8'6—dc22

                                                                    2008049266

ISBN-13: 978-1-59253-518-7
ISBN-10: 1-59253-518-6

10 9 8 7 6 5 4 3 2 1

Cover Design: Collaborated
Layout & Production: Megan Cooney
Photographs: Glenn Scott Photography, pages 1–89 and page 111; Timothy S. Allen, pages 90, 102, and 103; India Flint, pages 92–93; Abigail Doan, pages 94–95, Jean-Yves Vigneau, pages 96–97; Cat Collier, pages 98–99; Jennifer Khoshbin, pages 100–101; Jane Ingram Allen, pages 102–103; Susan Lenart Kazmer, pages 104–105; Bryant Holsenbeck, pages 106–107; Jana Trent, pages 108–109; Nina Bagley, pages 112–113; Lauren Ferguson, pages 114–115; Deedra Ludwig, pages 116–117; Jude Hill, pages 118–119; and Basia Irland, pages 120–123

Printed in China

This book is dedicated to my mom,
for all she selflessly gave me in life and spirit,
and to my son, Nico.
I hope to do the same for him.

Handmade paint on repurposed wood

IF I KEEP A GREEN BOUGH IN MY HEART,
THE SINGING BIRD WILL COME.

-LAO-TZU

INTRODUCTION

The inspiration for this book came about on my journey toward trying to make more mindful choices for my artwork and to walk upon the Earth as gently as possible.

As an artist, I am passionate about the creative process. In art school, I was so excited about being in a studio environment and painting all day that the dazed feeling I had after class—the result of so many students working with solvents in poorly ventilated studios—didn't even faze me. I remember wiping my oil paint brushes on my jeans and painting with oils in my studio apartment, not far from where I slept. I often handled questionable art materials with my bare hands and, for many years, used art materials in unconventional ways without really considering the consequences.

Things changed when I started paying attention to our global environmental crisis and especially when I became pregnant. Not only did I begin to examine the products I used in my home and on my body, I also took a hard look at my art supply shelves. How did the materials I used in my art affect not only my immediate environment but the environment at large? What kind of world was I creating and leaving for my child? These questions sparked my interest in learning more about art materials and about how I, as both artist and consumer, could make better choices.

Every choice we make about art supplies matters. For example, many oil paints and solvents contain petrochemicals, and even acrylic paints can contain toxic heavy metals and biocides, which can pollute our home environment and seep into our groundwater.

From recipes concocted in their own studios, artists of the past created astounding works of art that have sustained to this day. We can do the same. We can create wonderful art pieces from materials that leave little or no impact on the environment and, if used properly, won't compromise our long-term health.

While doing research for this book, I came to realize that many people view the "Green Movement" as a marketing tool, created to get consumers to choose certain products over others. This movement is really a revolution about consuming less, reusing more, and being mindful about the impact our choices have on the environment and on our health.

Making the decision to "go green" in art making will mean different things to different people. For some, it might mean making their own paints; others might choose to eliminate certain colors from their paint palettes or use scrap wood for a canvas. No change is too small or insignificant; even the little changes we make every day add up. My goal is to inspire you to examine your art-making process and make room for some greener choices. If these greener choices work for you, pass the knowledge on!

peace

This tree was created using
papers from the recycle bin

THE TREE WHICH MOVES SOME TO TEARS OF JOY IS IN THE
EYES OF OTHERS ONLY A GREEN THING THAT STANDS IN THE
WAY. SOME SEE NATURE ALL RIDICULE AND DEFORMITY . . .
AND SOME SCARCE SEE NATURE AT ALL. BUT TO THE EYES OF
THE MAN OF IMAGINATION, NATURE IS IMAGINATION ITSELF.

-WILLIAM BLAKE

CHAPTER 1

GREENING YOUR STUDIO

A trip to the art-supply store can be exciting—the shelves are packed with lots of products that inspire us to spend, spend, spend! But think before you pull out that wallet. From the moment we step into the art supply store and choose which of the dizzying array of products to spend our money on, we exert our power as consumers. When we choose green art supplies and avoid toxic products, we send a direct message to both the retailers and the manufacturers about what we, as artists, want in our studios.

Some manufactures are testing the waters by offering green alternatives alongside their regular product lines. When we choose the products that are safe for us and for the environment, we let these forward-thinking manufacturers know that we are conscious consumers and that we are paying attention. We encourage them to offer materials such as nontoxic paints and tree-free papers. When we avoid buying from manufacturers of toxic products, we're sending them the message that they need to change if they want our business. If you discover a manufacturer that is making positive changes, send the company an email and say thanks! Then let your local retailer know that you want to see green alternatives in the art-supply section.

But encouraging manufacturers to go green is only half the equation; we also need to make changes in the way *we* think and work. Before you head out to the art or craft store, ask yourself if you really need new "stuff." Can you create those gorgeous papers and cool embellishments from items you already have around your home or studio? Maybe you could throw a swap party and trade some of the products you've barely—or never—used with other artist friends. If you absolutely must have that new set of pens or paint color, ask yourself if using it poses health or environmental risks. Is there a greener alternative? Note the packaging: Is it excessive or recyclable? Can it be repurposed? Help balance your consumption by bringing a canvas tote bag or riding your bike or using public transportation to get to the art store.

We have become very comfortable as a disposable society; we're only slowly becoming conscious of the reality that things don't magically disappear when we put them into the trash can. Turning items that no longer serve their purpose into new tools and art-making materials keeps them out of the landfill. Can that Chinese food container be washed and used to store rubber stamps? Maybe that empty candy tin can hold sewing needles or tacks. Think before you toss. Just taking proper care of our materials helps by reducing consumption. When we take care of our tools, they last longer, and when they last longer, they don't need to be replaced as often.

You don't have to go to extremes to go green; start with the simple things. Remember, even the small choices we make each day can make a difference.

PRODUCT SAFETY

A good way to start the greening process in your studio is to find out which of the goods on your shelves are safe and eco-friendly. The easiest way to do this is to read the instructions and handling information for each product, paying special attention to any warning labels. The labels will give you the best insight into exactly what you are working with.

To determine whether a product is nontoxic, look for the AP (Approved Product) seal of the Art & Creative Materials Institute, Inc. (ACMI). The ACMI, a non-profit association of manufacturers of art, craft, and other creative materials, has been testing products since 1940. Member manufacturers voluntarily submit their products for review by the ACMI toxicology team, and, in turn, the ACMI certifies that the products carry the appropriate health warning labels.

The ACMI's team of toxicologists reviews each product, evaluating the following:

* each ingredient and its quantity
* possible adverse interaction with other ingredients
* the product's size and packaging
* potential acute and chronic harm to any part of the human body
* possible allergic reaction
* how a product is commonly used and misused
* U.S. national and state labeling regulations
  (Source: ACMI website.)

Products carrying the AP seal are certified to be nontoxic and, as stated on the ACMI website, are safe for both children and adults, because the toxicology team bases its evaluation on the use and misuse (such as ingesting a material) of the product by a small child. Some nontoxic products might bear older ACMI seals, such as such as CP (Certified Product) and HL Health Label (Non-Toxic); these are being replaced by the AP seal.

Not all the materials the ACMI certifies are nontoxic, however. Some carry the CL seal, which means that the product *can* contain hazardous materials. (See below.) The CL seal replaces the HL Health Label (Cautions Required), which you might still find on some products. Products bearing any of the ACMI seals are also certified to comply to ASTM D 4236 and the U.S. Labeling of Hazardous Art Materials Act (LHAMA). (Source: ACMI website.)

To find out what the labels on your products mean or whether a product is nontoxic, check out the ACMI website at www.acminet.org. The site provides a searchable certified product list.

. . . .

The AP seal "is found on products that contain no materials in sufficient quantities to be toxic or injurious to humans or to cause acute or chronic health problems." (Source: ACMI website.)

The CL seal "is found on art materials for adults that are certified to be properly labeled for any known health risks and is accompanied by information on the safe and proper use of such materials." Consider this a cautionary label, stating that the product contains hazardous ingredients. (Source: ACMI website.)

. . . .

OTHER LABELS TO LOOK FOR

If a product does not carry an ACMI seal and isn't listed in the ACMI certified products list, the manufacturer is not an ACMI member and other product labeling might be used.

One label you are likely to see comes from the Labeling of Hazardous Art Materials Act (LHAMA), which states that manufacturers of art supplies must test and label products for long-term health effects such as cancer and brain damage. Products that have been tested and labeled according to this law bear a label stating "Conforms with ASTM D 4236."

To find out more information about a product not carrying an ACMI seal, visit the manufacturer's website and look for its Material Safety Data Sheets (MSDS). These Data Sheets provide a wealth of product details, including composition, health hazards, first aid measures, storage and handling, ecological information, and safe disposal methods. Some manufacturers do not provide Data Sheets for their products, but do provide health and safety information.

Another label you might see is a Proposition 65 warning label. California's Proposition 65, also known as the Safe Drinking Water and Toxic Enforcement Act of 1986, enforces the labeling of hazardous products sold in the state of California. If a product contains substances classified as toxins, it must carry a variation of the following label: "WARNING: This product contains chemicals known to the State of California to cause cancer and birth defects or other reproductive harm."

To view a list of the chemicals classified as hazardous (updated yearly), visit California's Office of Environmental Health Hazard Assessment (OEHHA) at www.oehha.ca.gov/prop65.html.

If you can't find any safety information for a product, by all means, contact the manufacturer with your questions and concerns. When you tell the folks making your favorite products that these issues are important to you, they will see that there is a growing market for cleaner and greener art materials.

IS IT EARTH-FRIENDLY?

Now for the bad news: Just because a product is nontoxic doesn't mean it's Earth-friendly.

Unfortunately, many products labeled nontoxic emit volatile organic compounds (VOCs) that not only cause headaches and dizziness when inhaled but can contribute (little by little) to the destructive forces of greenhouse gases. And even low- or no-VOC products can harm the environment if they are disposed of improperly—in other words, by dumping them down the drain or throwing them into the trash. And here's another thing to consider: Although certain chemicals may not be delivered in toxic doses in specific products, cumulatively, these chemicals might be harmful to the Earth.

If a label states that the product presents a danger to your health, chances are good that it also presents a danger to the groundwater. Read product labels and follow the instructions to be sure that you dispose of waste properly. (For more on proper disposal of art materials, see page 19.)

- -

REPURPOSING IN THE STUDIO

- -

* Old credit cards and library cards are great for applying heavy paint layers and adhesives.
* Cut grooves into the end of cardboard pieces to create interesting marks in a wet painted surface.
* Egg cartons make perfect paint palettes.
* Save old chopsticks, sharpen the ends in a pencil sharpener, and use them for marking in wet paint or applying inks to the surface of your art.
* Old or scratched sheets of Plexiglas from picture frames make great cutting boards.

PAINTS AND MEDIUMS

People have been using paint to express themselves for some 30,000 years. Back then, without the local art-supply store to turn to, the world's earliest artists relied on natural ingredients for their paint recipes. In Africa, France, and Spain, for example, cave-painters mixed mineral pigments and burned bones with blood and animal fat to depict charging bulls, rhinos, and hunters. In the centuries that followed, artists explored the potential of a wide variety of ingredients, such as tree bark, insects, eggs, and milk, to make various binders for the pigments.

By the fifteenth century, oil paints were being developed, and artists experimented and refined their recipes extensively, using walnut, poppy seed, hemp seed, and castor and linseed oils in their paints. Unfortunately, these paints required toxic solvents, such as mineral spirits, for cleanup. By the 1840s, with the invention of the airtight paint tube, artists no longer had to make paints themselves, and the process of controlling paint ingredients began to lose out to convenience. Increasingly, over the centuries, paint recipes changed to include potentially toxic ingredients, such as preservatives to extend a paint's shelf life and other chemicals to give the paint a better texture. These additives were used not just for oil paints but for acrylics, too.

Today, many artists are looking for healthier alternatives to toxic paints; they're passing on synthetic, commercially manufactured paints and turning to natural pigments ground from minerals and dug up from the earth. But even natural pigments have a dark side. Some natural mineral pigments, such as those containing cadmium, copper, or chromium, are highly toxic and can cause serious health problems. Fortunately, the rise of natural, eco-friendly pigment suppliers has made using nontoxic natural pigments safer and easier.

To find out more about the hazards of working with pigments, binders, and numerous other artist materials, visit www.ci.tucson.az.us/arthazards, an excellent website from the city of Tucson, which provides an extremely comprehensive database.

SOLVENTS

Although many paints and mediums are, in themselves, not toxic, they can become toxic to you and to the environment if they require solvents for use and cleanup. Oil, enamel, and epoxy paints fit into this category and pose a hazard if these solvents are improperly handled. Most solvents, particularly turpentine, emit VOCs, and studies show that short-term exposure to these VOCs can cause headaches, nausea, and skin irritations. Long-term exposure can lead to cancer and damage to the liver, kidney, and central nervous system.

If using solvents is a necessary element of your art-making process, be sure that your workspace has a window exhaust fan and that you wear protective neoprene gloves; you might even want to get yourself a respirator.

Better still, avoid using turpentine mineral spirits, if possible, and try a citrus-based alternative. Citrus solvents (not to be confused with citrus-based household cleaners) are made from the oils of citrus peels, a biodegradable renewable resource, and offer the same performance as turpentine and other mineral spirits. Citrus solvents give off a citrus smell that is not harmful to your lungs or to the air. Companies such as the Real Milk Paint Company, Earthpaint, and Eco-House offer pure citrus solvent, and you can probably find it at your local art supply or hardware store, as well.

To avoid using solvents altogether, stick with water-based paints and mediums, such as acrylics, milk paints, gouache, and watercolor. You might also give the new water-mixable oil paints a try. Because these paints clean up and mix with water, they eliminate the need for solvents.

ACRYLIC PAINTS

Acrylic paints are considered a modern alternative to oil paints (with the exception of drying time—acrylics dry much faster) and clean up easily with water. However not all artists' acrylics are nontoxic. Some pigments contain toxic heavy metals, such as cadmium and even lead, which can be hazardous to your health and to the environment. Unfortunately, acrylic paints also rely on the petrochemical industry for their acrylic polymer emulsions, which are used as binders. As much as 36 billion pounds (16 billion kg) of toxic polymer solvents are produced annually and many of these are found in our art supplies. (Source: *Science Daily*, 2001.)

While most acrylic paint manufacturers offer a wide range of beautiful nontoxic color palettes, keep in mind that the majority of these paints (regardless of whether the label reads nontoxic) do emit VOCs, which generally come from the preservatives added to keep the paints from spoiling and freezing.

There's good news, though. At least one manufacturer has come up with Earth-friendly acrylic paints that are VOC- and solvent-free and made from organic pigments. With its "Green Art" line of products, Loew-Cornell has become a pioneer in providing green art supplies. The company even uses recycled aluminum for the paint tubes and recycled paper for the packaging. Paintbrush sets are made from reclaimed wood handles, recycled metal ferrules, and animal-free brush hair. Loew-Cornell pencil sets are made from recycled wood and organic pigments, its table easels and lap desks from recycled wood, and its oil pastels are organic and nontoxic. If the line gains support, perhaps we will see the company develop more products.

LATEX PAINT

One alternative to acrylic paints can be found in your hardware store. In response to the demand for eco-friendly house paints, manufacturers such as Sherwin-Williams, Benjamin Moore, General Paint, and others have been busy developing no- and low-VOC latex paints. These paints can yield similar results to artists' acrylics.

A number of modern and contemporary painters, including Jean Michel-Basquiat, have used latex in their paintings. If you're worried about its archival qualities, note that artists who have been using it for decades claim that their work is aging just fine. Purists, however, don't agree. The issue remains debatable, but if the paint is used on a well-stretched and primed canvas or wood panel, kept in a protective environment, it should last a long time. Try it out for yourself and see what you think. You can find low- and no-VOC latex house paints in small jars, which are perfect for experimentation. A note of caution, however: Adding a commercial color to no- and low-VOC paints will cause the VOC levels to rise, unless the pigment is also no-VOC. VOC levels are higher in dark colors than in light colors. For a list of zero- and low-VOC paint manufacturers, go to http://delta-institute .org/publications/paint.pdf. There is a great chart here: www .tucsonaz.gov/arthazards. Created by the city of Tucson, this chart gives a very thorough list.

MILK PAINT

For a nontoxic and environmentally friendly paint, try milk paint. Milk paint, which has been around for centuries, is making a comeback, gaining mainstream attention for its eco-friendliness. Many artists have begun experimenting with milk paint, because it produces results similar to acrylic paints.

You can make your own milk paint (see Chapter 2 for recipe), or you can buy powdered milk paint from companies such as the Old Fashioned Milk Paint Company and the Real Milk Paint Company. These paints are permanent, nontoxic, earth-friendly, and are packaged in simple, brown paper bags or cardboard. They are also free of VOCs, HAPs (hazardous air pollutants), lead, mercury, radioactive materials, petroleum byproducts, plastics, synthetic preservatives, and solvents or poisons of any kind. They are also noncombustible. Although preparing your paints might take a few moments (just add water to the powder and mix), knowing that there are no consequences to your creativity should lend a peace of mind that is worth those extra minutes.

OTHER PAINT OPTIONS

Watercolors, gouache, and casein paints can be eco-friendly choices, because the binders in these paints come from renewable resources; casein is a milk product, and the binder in watercolor and gouache is gum arabic, harvested from acacia trees. Just be sure to check the labels and avoid the toxic pigment colors. Because these paints are water-soluble, they clean up easily with water.

MAKING THE MOST OF YOUR PAINTS, MEDIUMS, AND TOOLS

Conserving the materials you already have helps reduce consumption and reduces waste, so it is an important step in keeping your studio green. To get the most out of your paints and mediums, proper storage is key. When you open a paint or medium container for the first time, cut an old plastic bag to the diameter of the opening plus 2" to come around the edge of the container. After each use, place the plastic over the opening before closing the lid to keep out air and help the paint last longer. Store bottled paints and mediums with flip-tops upside down (be sure the lids are tightly closed) to get the maximum amount of paint from each bottle, letting gravity do the work. Also remember to store your paints in a cool, dry area, away from heaters and sunny areas.

When it comes to greening the studio, you don't need to toss all your paints into the trash; just use them mindfully, and, when it comes time to freshen up your supplies, choose greener options. Remember, the more effort you make to let the manufacturers of your favorite materials know that you want more eco-friendly product choices, the more likely it is that we'll see a change.

BRUSH CARE

Another way to keep your studio eco-friendly is by taking care of your tools. Paintbrushes can be one of our biggest expenses, and proper care can ensure our brushes a long and well-used lifetime.

* Avoid letting paint and mediums dry on your brushes! Wipe, then rinse your brushes immediately in warm water after use.
* Don't leave your brushes soaking in water for too long; soaking loosens the hairs and can even distort the paintbrush handle.
* When you are finished with your brushes for the day, wash them with soap and warm water. Castile soap, which does not contain harsh chemicals, is a good choice.
* Dry and store your brushes upright, so the bristles aren't crushed.

HOW TO PROPERLY DISPOSE OF ART MATERIALS

If you work with oil paints, you know that used turpentine and even the rags you work with are flammable and need to be disposed of as hazardous waste materials. Contact your local sanitation department to find out the location of the nearest drop-off depot.

Another concern for artists is whether you can truly just dump the dirty wash water for water-soluble paints, mediums, and adhesives down the sink drain. Most paint manufacturers state that it is perfectly fine to dispose of minimal amounts (the paint use of the average artist) this way. Although water treatment plants can generally control these small amounts of paint waste, it's good to be in the habit of wiping excess paint off of brushes, tools, and surfaces with an old rag before rinsing them in the wash water, so you aren't tossing excessive amounts of paint waste down the drain. If you don't want to dump wastewater down the drain, check out the Golden Artist Colors, Inc., website for a simple tutorial on removing water-based paint solids from rinse water. (See the Resource guide on page 124.)

Paint manufacturers also suggest that small quantities of water-based paints and mediums require no special disposal methods, other than letting the paint dry before tossing it into the garbage. Larger paint quantities, however, require special disposal services. Visit www.earth911.org to find out the locations of these drop-off depots in your community. You can also donate larger quantities of latex paints to your local Habitat for Humanity for projects within your community.

ADHESIVES

Finding a strong, versatile, eco-friendly, and VOC-free adhesive can be a challenge. Although many common glues and mediums are labeled nontoxic (many even carry the ACMI AP seal), they do emit VOCs to some degree. A good all-purpose, eco-friendly alternative to mainstream adhesives, for use in everything from collage to assemblage, is EcoGlue. EcoGlue is also available in an animal-free formula specifically designed for wood projects, and, for heavy-duty projects involving stones, metals, and glass, the same company also makes EcoGlue Extreme.

Gorilla Glue (no, it's not made from gorillas; it's just super strong) is another option. It is both nontoxic and VOC-free and can be found at art supplies and hardware stores in a variety of sizes, depending on your needs. Another versatile glue is Weldbond universal adhesive, which is also vegan. And for a good glue stick to keep in your art journal bag for art making on the go, Coccoina offers a nontoxic, solvent- and acid-free glue stick made from all-natural ingredients such as potato starch and almond oil.

PAPER

Artists adore working with paper, whether they're building books, creating journals, or using patterned papers in collages and myriad other art projects. Buying paper can be positively addictive. Unfortunately, our addiction to paper comes with devastating consequences: the destruction of the world's forests; water pollution from chemical run-off; millions of tons of paper waste in the landfills. The pulp and paper industry is one of the largest consumers of energy and water and a huge contributor of greenhouse-gas emissions. All this to make that gorgeous piece of decorative paper that you just can't resist.

What's a paper lover to do? Well, you can make your own paper, from nontoxic, natural materials, or you can look for re-cycled and tree-free papers, which are gentle on the environment. Lots of wonderful papers are made from 100-percent recycled paper and from hemp, flax, cotton, and even recycled denim! You can also recycle the papers lurking around your studio. Reuse papers by painting over them or slicing up old drawings and paint-ings to use in new ones. After all, not everything we create is a masterpiece that must be saved forever—reuse it! Your junk mail pile can also be a good source for collage papers. The insides of security envelopes often have interesting designs, and old news-print can be saved for papier-mâché work.

LET'S HEAR IT FOR HEMP!

Strong and durable, hemp fiber is used to make sail cloth, paper, rope, and canvas; it was also the fabric of choice for Betsy Ross's American flag and the paper of choice for both the Declaration of Independence and the Bill of Rights. Hemp cloth is stronger than cotton and, unlike cotton, its production does not require the heavy use of pesticides. Hemp paper is naturally acid-free and requires less processing than wood paper.

If you are worried about the narcotic properties of hemp, rest assured, you won't be getting high in the studio. Industrial hemp (*Cannabis sativa*) and marijuana are different plant varieties. Hemp contains low THC (tetrahydrocannabinol) levels, which makes it unusable as a psychoactive drug.

What makes hemp so green is that, as a fast-growing plant, it is a clean, renewable resource that produces more fiber per acre than any other fiber-producing plant. It is also beneficial to the soil. Hemp is being explored for use in building and construction materials, nutritional goods, and even as a clean alternative fuel.

CANVAS

A stretched canvas is always a treat to work on, especially for painting. But when it comes to being green, pre-stretched canvases don't offer much choice. The solution? Stretch your own canvases. You not only save money, you reduce waste and reduce consumption. You also have more control over the materials you use, such as stretcher bars made from sustainable wood and canvases made from unbleached, organic cotton, hemp, or linen. You can find beautiful organic cotton and hemp blends, which provide a wonderful painting surface. Or go through your fabric stash and stretch a canvas made from recycled fabric. Stretching your own canvases is easier than you might think. To find out how, see Chapter 3, page 66.

Another option for reducing the need for new canvases is to rework or paint over old paintings. If an older piece of art is no longer working for you, just paint a few fresh coats of gesso on top and create something new.

Canvas panels, which provide a stable surface for painting and mixed media, can also be a green choice. Look for panels with inner boards made from 100-percent recycled and acid-free materials.

SAFETY IN THE STUDIO

According to the U.S. Environmental Protection Agency, "in the last several years, a growing body of scientific evidence has indicated that the air within homes and other buildings can be more seriously polluted than the outdoor air in even the largest and most industrialized cities. Other research indicates that people spend approximately 90 percent of their time indoors. Thus, for many people, the risks to health may be greater due to exposure to air pollution indoors than outdoors."

We consider our homes to be our sanctuaries and our workspaces to be conduits for our self-expression. Indoor air pollution is yet another work hazard, and artists are even more at risk if their art materials contain hazardous materials or are handled incorrectly. Make sure your workspace is well ventilated and that all your paint and medium materials are stored in a cool dry place, clearly labeled and closed tightly. If your studio does not have adequate ventilation, consider using an energy-efficient air purifier to filter particle matters from your workspace. If you have little ones who frequent your studio, keep questionable items up on a shelf and out of reach.

SAFE STUDIO TIPS

* Wear a face mask when using spray products.
* If possible, avoid skin contact with materials.
* Allow paint rags to dry completely before disposing them.
* Wash your studio clothes separately from your regular clothes. It's also a good idea to keep your work clothes in the studio, so you can easily change into and out of them.
* Wash your hands when you are finished in the studio.
* Vacuum—don't sweep—work areas.
* Keep the National Poison Control Number handy for emergencies: 1-800-222-1222.

FORGET NOT THAT THE EARTH DELIGHTS
    TO FEEL YOUR BARE FEET
        AND THE WINDS LONG TO PLAY WITH YOUR HAIR.

                -KAHLIL GIBRAN

CHAPTER 2

GREEN RECIPES

Making your own art materials puts you in complete control of the ingredients you use in your art-making process and can help create a closer connection between you, your hand-mixed materials, and the finished work of art. By mixing up the age-old, time-proven recipes provided in this chapter, you can avoid using animal- or petrochemical-based paints. Many commercially manufactured paints, whether they are acrylic, oil, or latex, contain biocides, including formaldehyde, which can off-gas long after the paint is dry. Biocides, chemicals used to kill biological organisms, are used in paints to extend the shelf life of the paint and preserve the ingredients. When you make your own paints on demand—whether from manufactured earth pigments or colors you've created from natural ingredients—you eliminate the need for these preservatives and reduce your exposure to nasty chemicals.

Making your own adhesives also helps you control the chemicals you come in contact with, and you might be surprised how simple some reliable glue recipes can be! Experiment with these recipes to make them work for you.

Remember to wear a face mask when dealing with powdered pigments and ingredients, to avoid breathing in particles, and be sure your work space is well ventilated. Wearing a pair of impervious work gloves when mixing your recipes also helps limit unnecessary contact with materials, even if they are considered nontoxic. Be sure to clearly label your jars and stored mixtures; include the date on the label to keep track of the mixtures' lifespan. Lastly, keep mixtures in an area that is inaccessible to kids or pets!

As you experiment with making your own paints and adhesives, document your results in an art journal or sketch book (or create your own recipe journal), citing the recipe, ingredients, and dates, and including a color or glue swatch. A journal will help you remember the results of the various formulas. It can also be a helpful tool for recording the lightfastness of various plant dyes.

MAKING PAINT

To mix your own paints, all you need is pigment, some form of glue to act as a binder, and a mixing bowl. I'll discuss the two central ingredients first; the recipes will follow. Many of these recipes have been simplified as much as possible to help make the paint-making process more appealing and accessible.

PIGMENTS

Pigments are the matter that adds color to paints. Historically, pigments were derived from clays, minerals, plant life, and even burned animal bones. Many of these earth pigments, still vibrant on ancient cave walls and cliff dwellings, have stood the test of time and offer colors that are unmatched by their modern synthetic alternatives, many of which contain heavy metals such as chromium, cadmium, and arsenic and which can pose serious health risks upon excessive exposure. These are chemicals you should avoid dumping down the sink with the brush water. (See How to Properly Dispose of Art Materials, page 19.)

Keep in mind, however, that not all naturally occurring pigments are necessarily nontoxic. Some natural pigments can contain other minerals that require additional caution. Orpiment (used to make canary yellow), for example, contains highly toxic arsenic, and Egyptian blue contains copper, which can be toxic if inhaled or ingested. Powdered-pigment suppliers generally provide details of their pigments' toxicity and the risks associated with them on their websites and in their catalogs. Two very informative sources for detailed information on pigments are the websites of the Natural Pigments (www.naturalpigments.com) and Earth Pigments (www.earthpigments.com) companies. The Earth Pigments Company also states that its pigments are environmentally safe, nontoxic, and extracted using environmentally sound mining practices. When purchasing pigments, don't hesitate to ask if the distributor's sources practice environmentally

responsible mining. Chances are that if they do, the company will be more than happy to let you know.

Some pigments are more lightfast than others. Mineral pigments, for example, tend to be more lightfast than natural plant pigments. To find out how lightfast your pigments are, try a simple, low-tech home test. Mix up your paint recipe and paint a page in your art journal or sketchbook. Once the page is dry, tear the page in half and place the torn half in a sunny location. (Tape it to a wall that gets lots of sun, for example, or even to a window.) Keep the other half enclosed in your journal. Monitor the swatch every couple of weeks by comparing it to the other half of the paper in your journal. For the best results, wait a couple of months and note the difference between the two swatches.

Following is a list of some natural earth pigment colors that are available in powdered form and are considered safe for your health and the environment when handled properly (using a face mask and gloves in a well-ventilated work space). Although these pigments are natural, be sure to use them with care. Keep them clearly labeled and away from children and pets, and dispose of them properly.

* Red: red iron oxide (hematite), red ochers
* Yellows: yellow ochers
* Green: green earth (celadonite), Nicosia green earth, cold green earth (glauconite)
* Blue: lapis lazuli, blue ochre (vivianite)
* Violet: caput mortum violet (cold hematite)
* Brown: burnt sienna, raw sienna, burnt umber*, raw umber*
* Black: carbon black (Shungite), bone black, black oxide
* White: titanium white, calcium carbonate (egg shells!)
* Magical effects: mica powder adds a beautiful sparkly shine!

NOTE: *Umber itself is not toxic, but it can contain manganese, which is toxic if inhaled or ingested.

You can also discover your own earth pigments, by digging deep into the soil of your backyard or neighborhood. You might find variations in clay colors, from red to deep brown. To harvest these colors, dig them up and remove any large pieces of rock, sticks, or debris, then allow the earth to dry in a sunny location. Once dry, sift out the smaller debris with a fine kitchen strainer and use a mortar and pestle to grind the earth to a fine powder. The resulting pigment can be mixed into your choice of binders (see page 30).

PLANT AND VEGETABLE DYES

Plant and vegetable dyes offer the greenest choice of all—paints from renewable resources. Why not explore the potential paints found in your kitchen or backyard garden? Although many plant and vegetable dyes are not very lightfast, meaning they won't hold their original color when exposed to sunlight for long periods of time (for more on lightfastness, see page 24), they can still be fun to play and experiment with, and they work well on the protected pages of art journals and altered books.

To derive a dye from a plant, first find your paint source and boil it in a pot of water. As a general guideline, the ratio is 1 part plant or vegetable material to approximately 8 parts water. Bring the ingredients to a boil for an hour. As the dye develops, test the color with a paintbrush on a piece of white paper. You might even want to create a journal of your recipes, documenting the plant or vegetable name and the corresponding preparation times for each sample.

See the following page for a list of some of the colors plants and fruits can yield. Don't be afraid to experiment with these plant dyes—add them to different binders for interesting results!

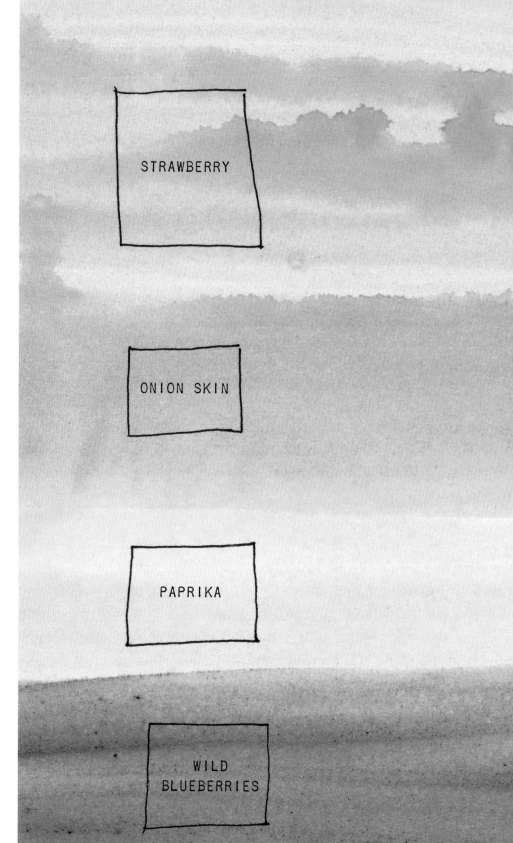

STRAWBERRY

ONION SKIN

PAPRIKA

WILD BLUEBERRIES

RED

MADDER
STRAWBERRIES
CHERRIES
HIBISCUS FLOWERS
BEETS
ROSE HIPS
HENNA

YELLOW AND ORANGE

ANNATTO SEED POWDER
SAFFRON
TURMERIC ROOT
DANDELION FLOWERS

CUMIN

FIG LEAVES
BIRCH LEAVES
RAGWORT PLANT
MARIGOLD FLOWERS
PINE CONES

GREEN

GRASS
NETTLE
SPINACH
CRABAPPLE LEAVES

BLUE AND VIOLET

INDIGO (*INDIGOFERA*) LEAVES
WOAD (ALSO KNOWN AS DYERS
    WOAD) LEAVES
BLUEBERRIES
ELDERBERRIES
BLACKBERRIES
RED ONION SKINS

BROWN

ONION SKINS
WALNUT SHELLS
BLACK TEA
JUNIPER BERRIES
COFFEE GROUNDS
PAPRIKA

BINDERS

Binders, which can be made from animal, plant, or synthetic sources, hold the paint together. They also help to hold paint onto the canvas or other surface to which they're applied. Different binders yield different paint strengths, so choose your binders according to the surface you plan on painting. The following water-soluble binders do not require the use of solvents.

ANIMAL-BASED BINDERS
GELATIN

To make a gelatin binder, you can use food-grade gelatin, available at your local grocery store, or artist-grade gelatin from an art-supply store. Art stores generally carry gelatin in powdered and sheet forms. Both work fine. Gelatin can be used as a substitute for rabbit skin glue in some paint recipes and yields very similar results. Rabbit skin glue, essentially refined rabbit collagen, is a sizing that can be used as an adhesive and is an ingredient in traditional gesso. Although gelatin is an animal product (it's derived from cows), it is considered a "friendlier" alternative to rabbit skin glue—particularly for the rabbits!

Some companies manufacture organic food-grade gelatin, which can also be considered a friendlier choice, because the cows are fed a pesticide-free diet. Be aware, however, that "organic" does not necessarily mean that the cows are grazing in the sunshine all day. If this is important to you, contact the manufacturer to find out if the cows are sent to pasture. If consumers demand humane standards in animal food production, perhaps change will come about.

Eggs

Egg yolks serve as a strong paint binder in egg tempera paints. Used since medieval times in Europe, egg tempera is flexible, permanent, and does not yellow with age. Egg whites are used as a binder in glair paint, which is similar to watercolor, in that it is not permanent and has some transparency. The most ideal source for eggs is your local farmers' market or local chicken farmers who do not practice debeaking. If you don't have access to either, use organic cage-free eggs.

Casein

Casein (pronounced kay-seen) is a binder made from milk protein and dries with a smooth, velvet surface that is insoluble to water. I have been unable to find organic casein, but if this is a concern to you, contact casein powder manufacturers and let them know that this is a product you would support. If there is enough demand—especially with the rise of the popularity of organic milk—it might become available in the future.

TIP:
Save the egg shells for slaking into white pigment!

PLANT-BASED BINDERS
Gum Arabic

Harvested in Africa from the bark of acacia trees, gum arabic, also known as gum acacia, is a great water-based binder. It is stiff when dry, so gelatin or honey is usually added to make it flexible. A truly green choice for art making, gum arabic is a renewable resource, and increased demand for it helps support both reforestation and the social economics of rural African communities. Gum arabic, particularly the organic variety, is an animal-friendly, vegan alternative to animal-based binders.

Methyl Cellulose

Methyl cellulose, which is made from plant fibers, is another animal-friendly, vegan binder. It has long been used in the repair of delicate books and papers and is also the main ingredient in wallpaper paste. It comes in a powdered form; you simply add water. You can also use methyl cellulose as a sizing on paper in preparation for water media.

SYNTHETIC BINDERS
Acrylic Mediums

Acrylic medium is a polymer emulsion that, in its pure form, is nontoxic. It is water-based and extremely versatile as both a binder and an adhesive. However, many commercial acrylic mediums contain additives that emit VOCs, which, over the long term, can be dangerous to your health and to the environment. The Old Fashioned Milk Company makes a nontoxic, non-VOC acrylic medium called Extra-Bond, a concentrated polymer emulsion that's suitable as both a binder and as an adhesive in collage work.

To prevent the growth of bacteria and mold and avoid attracting bugs to your home-made recipes and artwork, add a few drops of an antibacterial or antifungal essential oil to your binders. The oils also add a nice smell to your work!

Essential oils that can be used as preservatives in homemade paints:

CITRONELLA

CLOVE

CINNAMON

EUCALYPTUS

JUNIPER

LAVENDER

LEMON

PEPPERMINT

ROSEMARY

SANDALWOOD

TEA TREE

THYME

WINTERGREEN

PAINT RECIPES

Many of these paint recipes have been used for hundreds of years. They are surprisingly easy to make, and the results are excellent. Just as in cooking, the recipes can be tweaked and adapted to suit your needs. Feel free to adjust and experiment with them to get the results you want. If a recipe calls for the use of a bowl, use a glass bowl instead of a metal bowl to avoid possible chemical reactions between the pigments and the metal.

All these recipes are water-based and safe, if the ingredients are handled correctly.

HELPFUL TOOLS

* Natural-pigment textures can vary, so have a mortar and pestle (below left) available to grind the powders, if necessary.
* Use a glass muller (below right) and glass plate or slab for thoroughly mixing paints.
* Use a palette knife to remove your blended paint mixtures from the slab.

TESTING YOUR RECIPES

Test your recipes by painting a test strip on a piece of paper. If the pigment rolls off when dry, you will need more binder. If it appears to be crackly, add more pigment.

WORKING WITH PIGMENTS

To use powdered pigments, mix your pigment with enough water to form a thick paste in a bowl or by using a glass muller on a glass slab before adding it to your paint recipe. This process is called slaking. Use a palette knife to remove the mixture from the slab.

. . . .
PIGMENT SAFETY
. . . .

When working with powdered pigments and mixing your own paint recipes, always remember to

* wear protective gear, including a dust mask and gloves,
* work in a well-ventilated area,
* mix your materials carefully, to avoid creating excessive dust,
* wash your hands after mixing recipes or working with materials,
* clearly label the containers you use for mixing and storing your pigments and paints, and
* keep your materials sealed tightly and store them away from children, pets, food, and drinks.

GELATIN GESSO

Gesso (pronounced je-so) is a primer that prepares your painting surface for paint and ensures that your paint adheres. Gesso can also make surfaces such as wood panels, paper scraps, and even metals (if cleaned and scored with sandpaper to create a tooth) into interesting canvases for your work.

INGREDIENTS

whiting (plaster of Paris
   or chalk)
gelatin
honey

INSTRUCTIONS

1. In a bowl, mix 1 part whiting with 1 part hot water.
2. In a separate bowl, add 1 part gelatin to 8 parts hot water. Stir until gelatin dissolves.
3. Add 1 part gelatin mix to 10 parts of the whiting mixture.
4. Add a few drops of warm honey.
5. Mix well. The mixture will thicken upon standing.

ADJUSTMENTS

* To make your gesso more flexible, add honey.
* To give it a heavier, more opaque body, add whiting.
* To thicken, add gelatin.
* To thin, add water.
* You can substitute casein binder (found in the casein paint recipe) for the gelatin-water mix. For a vegan alternative, substitute the gelatin-water mix with methyl cellulose glue.

APPLICATION

Apply gesso to raw canvas, paper, wood, or any other surface you want to paint. To get your surface completely white, you will need to apply two or three coats, applying each coat in alternate directions (vertical and horizontal). Store in an airtight jar.

ACRYLIC PAINT

Acrylic paint is a strong, fast-drying paint that is insoluble to water when dry. It can be used on most surfaces and can be thinned with water or additional acrylic medium.

INGREDIENTS

acrylic medium

pigment

INSTRUCTIONS

Combine 1 part acrylic medium and 1 part pigment by placing the acrylic medium on your palette and carefully adding the pigment.

ADJUSTMENTS

* For a smoother, more-transparent application, add more medium.
* For a more opaque application, add more pigment.
* Add water to adjust the consistency of the mixture.

APPLICATION

Apply acrylic paint thickly for a textured look and feel. To create transparent color washes, thin the paint with water and apply it in layers. Store your colors in airtight containers.

WATER-BASED BINDER FOR WATERCOLOR AND GOUACHE RECIPES

Watercolors and gouache are great for working on primed wood panels and papers and remain water-soluble even when dry.

INGREDIENTS

gum arabic

glycerin or honey (used as a plasticizer to keep the mix flexible)

essential oil preservative (see essential oils guide on page 33)

INSTRUCTIONS

1. In a bowl, mix 1 part gum arabic with 2 parts hot water.
2. Add 1 part glycerin to 5 parts of the gum arabic mix.
3. Add 2 drops of essential oil and mix well.

WATERCOLOR

Watercolor, also referred to by the French term *aquarelle*, dates back to the Renaissance. A water-based paint, its transparency is determined by the amount of water added to it. Watercolors allow you to build beautiful, transparent layers of color.

INGREDIENTS

water-based binder (see recipe on this page)

honey

pigment

INSTRUCTIONS

1. Mix 1 part honey with 9 parts water-based binder.
2. Mix 1 part binder-and-honey mixture with 1 part pigment to make a thick paste.

ADJUSTMENTS

* If the paste is too gritty, mix it on a glass slab with a muller.
* Paint can be thinned with water.

APPLICATION

Use this paint as you would any traditional watercolor, adding water to control its transparency. Store your colors in airtight containers. The mixtures will last about a year.

GOUACHE

An opaque, water-based paint, gouache (pronounced "gwash") dates back to sixteenth-century Europe. It has a heavier body than watercolor paints, due to the addition of white chalk pigment. Unlike watercolors, gouache colors are lightened by adding white gouache paint, rather than water. It offers a beautiful matte finish when dry.

INGREDIENTS

water-based binder
   (see recipe on page 38)
honey
pigment
whiting chalk

INSTRUCTIONS

1. Mix 1 part honey with 9 parts water-based binder.
2. Mix 1 part whiting chalk with 6 parts pigment.
3. Mix 1 part binder-and-honey mixture with 1 part pigment-and-whiting mixture to make a thick paste.

ADJUSTMENTS

* If gouache is too gritty, mix it on a glass slab with a muller.
* Paint can be thinned with water.

APPLICATION

Use this as you would watercolor paint, but add white gouache paint to create color variations. Store your colors in airtight containers. The mixtures will last about a year.

EGG TEMPERA PAINT

Because egg tempera paint is made with egg yolk, a perishable material, be sure to start with a fresh egg, and only make what you need, because it cannot be stored. Be sure also to avoid including the egg white, which speeds up the paint's drying process and therefore takes away from its smooth application. Don't worry if the yellow of the yolk appears to interfere with your color; the yellow cast will fade away after a day or so. If desired, you can add a couple of drops of white vinegar per yolk to your paint to act as a mild preservative.

INGREDIENTS

egg yolk (consider buying organic, cage-free eggs)
pigment

INSTRUCTIONS

1. Separate the yoke from the egg white and place the yolk in a glass bowl.
2. Remove the outer skin of the yolk. (Letting it dry for a few moments can make this process easier.) Puncture the yolk with your fingers or a small knife and pour the yolk into a small bowl or container.
3. Mix 1 part pigment with 1 part yolk binder.

ADJUSTMENTS

* If the paint is too thick, add a few drops of water.
* If the paint is gritty, mix it on a glass slab with a muller.

APPLICATION

Be sure each coat of paint is dry before adding the next coat, to avoid pulling up the layers underneath. This paint cannot be stored, so make only as much as is needed.

NOTE: When you are finished with your painting, varnish it after a few months with a whipped egg white (recipe follows).

EGG WHITE VARNISH RECIPE

1. Whip one egg white until it thickens.
2. Place the whipped white in a glass container and cover it with water.
3. Cover the container and allow the white to sit overnight.
4. Remove the liquid that has accumulated on top of the white and use this as the varnish.

GLAIR PAINT

Glair paints were popularly used during the fifth century to create illuminated manuscripts. Because this paint is not very strong, it works best on paper within a book structure and is a nice fit for art journaling. Use the leftover egg white from the tempera recipe to make this paint.

INGREDIENTS

egg white

pigment

INSTRUCTIONS

1. Whip 1 egg white with a few drops of water until frothy.
2. Mix 1 part whipped egg white with 1 part pigment.

ADJUSTMENTS

* If the paint is gritty, mix it on a glass slab with a muller.
* Use as you would a watercolor paint, thinning with water if necessary.

APPLICATION

This paint works best on paper and for journals. It cannot be stored, so make only as much as you need.

MILK PAINT

Milk paint dates back to ancient Egypt and was used in the United States during the Colonial period, typically for painting barns and furniture.

INGREDIENTS

- 2 quarts (1.9 L) whole milk
- 1 cup (235 ml) vinegar (optional)
- 4 tablespoons (52 gr) hydrated lime (found at gardening supply stores) or borax (found in the laundry aisle or at art-supply stores)
- pigment

INSTRUCTIONS

1. Pour milk into a bowl and set aside to sour and curdle. To speed up the curdling process, add 1 cup (235 ml) vinegar to the milk and set aside overnight. Alternatively, you can place the milk and vinegar mix in a pot on the stove over low heat for about 5 to 10 minutes.

2. Scoop out curds with a spoon and place them in a strainer. If you curdled the milk with vinegar, you will need to rinse the vinegar off the curds.

3. Place curds in a clean bowl and slowly stir in lime or borax. Mix well to eliminate all lumps, adding water if the mixture is too thick. This is your milk-paint binder.

4. Using a separate container for each color, mix 1 part binder with 2 parts pigment. Use less pigment for transparent effects, more pigment for an opaque finish.

APPLICATION

Use milk paint as you would an acrylic paint on most paintable surfaces, such as wood panels, paper, and canvas. The mixture will last for about a week if refrigerated, so be sure to make only what is needed.

CASEIN PAINT

Casein paint dates back to Asian cave paintings and was used up until the Renaissance. It is considered a durable and reliable paint, but be forewarned—it does smell a little strange! Fortunately, the smell dissipates as the paint dries.

INGREDIENTS

- 2 tablespoons (30 g) casein powder
- 1 tablespoon (13 g) borax (from the laundry aisle or art supply store)
- water
- 1 ounce (28 g) pigment

INSTRUCTIONS

1. Mix casein powder with 5 ounces (150 ml) warm water and let set overnight. Discard the water that accumulates on the surface.
2. Mix borax with 4 ounces (120 ml) hot water and add mixture to casein and water mixture. This is your casein binder. Let mixture set for about an hour.
3. Place a spoonful of the binder in a glass bowl and add pigment. Mix well. Alternatively, place binder and pigment on a glass slab and mix with a glass muller.

APPLICATION

Apply casein paint as you would acrylic paint on most paintable surfaces, such as wood panels, paper, and canvas. Adding water to the paint creates an effect similar to watercolor. Mixtures last for approximately a week, if refrigerated, so make only what is needed.

This bird was painted on a gesso primed woodblock remnant using the casein paint recipe.

ADHESIVE RECIPES

Eco-friendly, nontoxic glues are easily made from ingredients found in your pantry.

SIMPLE COLLAGE GLUE

INGREDIENTS

¼ cup (125 g) non-self-rising wheat flour

¼ cup (50 g) sugar

½ teaspoon powdered alum

1¾ cups (425 ml) warm water

essential oil (see essential oils guide on page 33)

INSTRUCTIONS

1. In a stainless steel pot, combine flour, sugar, and powdered alum.
2. Add water and stir until there are no lumps.
3. Bring mixture to a low boil and continue stirring until it appears almost transparent.
4. Remove the pot from heat and add a few drops of essential oil.
5. Allow the mixture to cool. Pour mixture into a jar.

APPLICATION

Apply with a paintbrush. The glue can be stored for several months.

RICE PASTE

This heavy-bodied paste works well for adhering paper and objects. Because it does not dry completely clear, use it underneath papers and objects, where it can't be seen.

INGREDIENTS

¾ cup (95 g) rice flour
2 tablespoons (26 g) sugar
¾ cup (175 ml) warm water
essential oil (see essential oils guide on page 33)

INSTRUCTIONS

1. In a pot, combine rice flour, sugar, and water. Stir until there are no lumps.
2. Stir over low heat until mixture has thickened.
3. Remove from heat and mix in a few drops of essential oil.
4. Allow mixture to cool, then pour into a jar.

APPLICATION

Apply with a paintbrush. Because this paste is quite thick, you might want to use an old credit card to spread it. This glue can be stored for several months.

WATERPROOF GLUE

INGREDIENTS

5 teaspoons (23 g) unflavored gelatin
6 tablespoons (90 ml) boiling water
2 teaspoons (10 ml) vinegar
2 teaspoons (10 ml) glycerin
essential oil (see the essential oils guide on page 33)

INSTRUCTIONS

1. In a pot, over low heat, combine gelatin with water.
2. Stir until gelatin is completely dissolved.
3. Add vinegar and glycerin. Mix well.
4. Remove from heat and stir in a few drops of essential oil. Pour mixture into a jar.

APPLICATION

Apply with a paintbrush. Use this glue while it is warm, because it can gel when it cools off. To warm it, simply place the jar in a bowl of warm water until the mixture softens. The glue can be stored for several months.

METHYL CELLULOSE GLUE

INGREDIENTS
5 tablespoons (40 g) methyl cellulose powder
1 cup (235 ml) cold water

INSTRUCTIONS
1. In a bowl, combine methyl cellulose powder and water. Mix well.
2. When the powder is completely dissolved, add enough cold water to bring the mixture to one quart (946 ml). Let the mixture sit overnight, then pour into a jar.

APPLICATION
Apply with a paintbrush. This glue is not waterproof, so it is best used as a paper glue, perfect for art journaling! The mixture will last several months.

GUM ARABIC GLUE

INGREDIENTS:
gum arabic
glycerin or honey (used as a plasticizer to keep mix flexible)
clove oil (see the essential oils guide on page 33)

INSTRUCTIONS
1. In a bowl, mix 1 part gum arabic with 2 parts hot water.
2. Combine 1 part glycerin and 5 parts gum arabic mix.
3. Add 2 drops of clove oil and mix well. Pour mixture into a jar.

APPLICATION
Apply with a paintbrush. Gum arabic glue can be used as an all-purpose paper glue. The mixture will last about a year.

CASEIN GLUE

INGREDIENTS

2 tablespoons (30 g) casein
powder

5 ounces (150 ml) warm water

1 tablespoon (13 g) borax
(available from laundry aisle
or art supply stores)

½ cup (120 ml) hot water

INSTRUCTIONS

1. Mix casein powder with water
and let set overnight. Discard
the water that accumulates on
the surface.

2. Mix borax with water, then
add liquid to casein and water mixture. Stir well. Pour mixture
into a jar.

APPLICATION

Apply with a paintbrush. Casein glue can be used as an
all-purpose paper glue. The mixture will last for a week,
if refrigerated, so be sure to make only what is needed.

TIP:
Use leftover glue in the Casein Paint recipe on page 43.

ACRYLIC GLUE

Acrylic medium, which was discussed in the binders section, can
be used without any added ingredients as a perfect collage adhesive and sealant. Simply apply the medium with a brush.

ALL-PURPOSE CLEANER

When it's time to tidy up your workspace, use this eco-friendly
cleaner to keep your surfaces and work areas clean.

INGREDIENTS

1 tablespoon (13 g) borax (disinfects, bleaches, and deodorizes)

1 tablespoon (15 ml) liquid castile soap (cleans)

1 tablespoon (15 ml) lemon juice (removes grease)

1 quart (946 ml) warm water

INSTRUCTIONS

Mix ingredients together and use as you would any cleaner.

THE GOAL OF LIFE IS TO MAKE YOUR
        HEARTBEAT MATCH THE BEAT OF THE UNIVERSE,
            TO MATCH YOUR NATURE WITH NATURE.

                                -JOSEPH CAMPBELL

CHAPTER 3

GREEN PROJECTS

Reduce, reuse, and recycle is a philosophy that can be applied not just to your trash but in the studio as well. Got an inspiration? Chances are, you don't really need to buy something new to bring it to life. Leftover paper bits can be used in collage and papier-mâché projects, old notebooks can be made into juicy art journals, construction remnants can be turned into painting canvases, and plastic shopping bags can be made into a sturdy fabric. We are limited only by our imaginations.

Let the following projects spark inspiration and ideas for your own recycled and repurposed adventures.

This canvas has been recycled many times by painting over it again and again. In its current stage, low-VOC latex paints and gel pens were used to create the Tree of Life.

REPURPOSING UNUSED OBJECTS INTO ART

If prepared properly, almost any surface can be painted on, opening the door to repurposing unused objects into art. Soiled and well-worn surfaces should be cleaned to remove dust or residue. Glossy, slick, or rough surfaces might need to be buffed with a fine sheet of sandpaper. When buffing surfaces with sandpaper, wear a dust mask to protect yourself and counter-cross your strokes. It is also a good idea to apply a coat of gesso to the dry surface of the painting area; this creates a good starting point and shows your paint colors true to life.

This diminutive guitar could no longer hold a tune, so it was repurposed into art. Before heading to the art-supply store, examine what you already have on hand that might work as an alternative canvas.

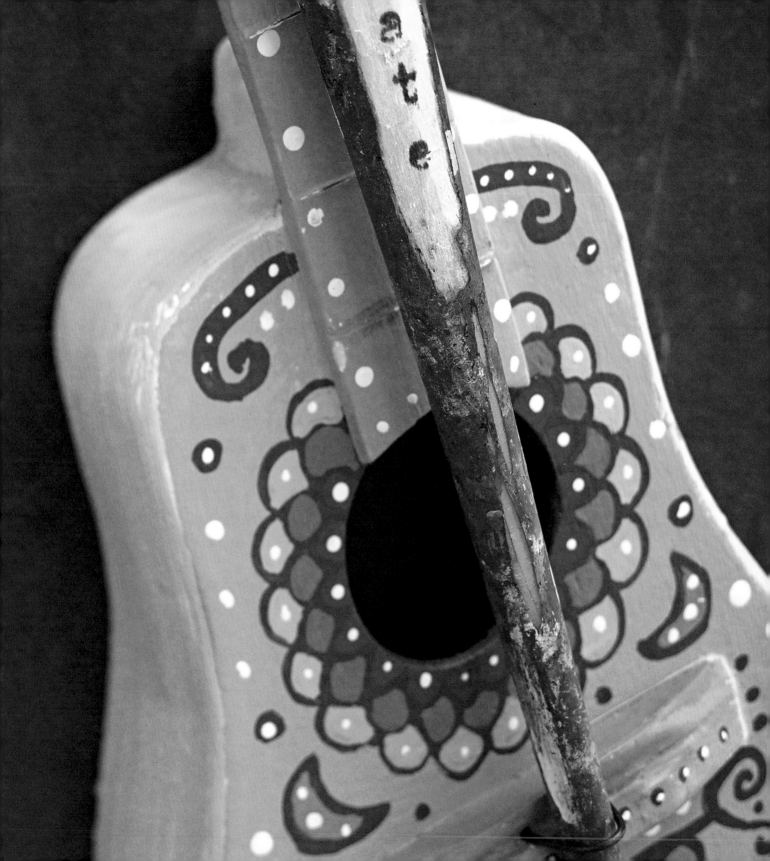

WOOD COLLAGE VIGNETTES

MATERIALS

remnant wood pieces in various sizes (for the background
   supports)

paint stirrers cut into smaller pieces (sizes and shapes
   are up to you)

your choice of paint (latex, acrylic, milk paint, gouache,
   watercolors)

adhesive

paper scraps

old photos

OPTIONAL:

die cuts

gel pens

nails

beads, buttons, washers, sequins, or other embellishments

Wood is a great material for mixed-media artists to work with: You can paint it, sand it, hammer it, and collage it without worrying about damaging the structure. Very rarely will you need to actually purchase new wood—remnant pieces from other people's construction projects are more accessible than you might think. Ask around; you might be surprised at what you can find in a friend's or neighbor's garage. What they consider to be scraps might serve as perfect supports for your artwork. If you don't have handy friends with wood scraps, visit or call your local lumber or hardware store and introduce yourself. Chances are, you can have scraps for free or at a minimal cost. Local thrift stores and yard sales can also yield some interesting wood objects that can be repurposed.

INSTRUCTIONS

FOR THE BASE:

1. Start with a wood block that will function as your base. The size and shape of the base are up to you.
2. Sand the edges to remove any rough edges or splinters, then prime the top and sides with two layers of gesso.
3. When the gesso is dry, apply a base color of paint. For these pieces, acrylic paint was used.

FOR THE WOOD COMPONENTS:

1. Old paint stirrers or wood rulers can be used for the smaller wood blocks. Cut the stirrers with a miter saw, or saw them by hand to the desired sizes. If you do not have access to a saw or power tools, try scoring the cut line with a craft knife, carefully working your way through the wood.
2. As you did for the larger wood block, sand the cut sides down to eliminate rough edges.
3. Prepare the small pieces by painting them with a base color.

FOR THE VIGNETTES:

1. Collage the small pieces, adding background images and other paper embellishments. It is easier to work with the wood pieces individually because you can easily trace and trim the background papers to specific sizes for each wood piece.
2. Lay out the collaged pieces before assembling the piece to see which ones work best alongside each other, changing them up as needed. Once you have a basic working design, you can begin to glue the blocks onto your larger base.

TIP:

Visual repetition can help create a powerful composition. Create hand-cut shapes or use a die cut for your repeating central images. Cutting parts from photographs can bring new life to your old photos and make your art even more personal.

ASSEMBLING THE WORK:

1. To glue the blocks to the base, use a paintbrush to apply a generous layer of acrylic medium or a glue from the recipes section to the back of each of the small blocks. Leave the assembled piece overnight to allow the glue to set.

2. When the glue is set, continue to collage, paint, and embellish the blocks. Gel pens and markers work well for doodling and drawing on top of the little collage blocks.

3. Once your collage and doodling is finished, seal the work with an acrylic medium and set to dry. When the top layer is dry, give the blocks a unified patina by painting over the entire piece with an acrylic or latex color (black works well), and then wipe it all off, allowing the paint to remain in the crevices.

4. For a finishing touch, hammer away! Small wire nails and upholstery tacks are great for embellishing wood. Add some beads, washers, sequins, buttons, or other findings to your nails before hammering them in, to add interesting visual elements.

5. Add a saw-tooth hanger to the back of the piece, and it's ready to be hung.

PAPIER-MÂCHÉ:
A FRESH LOOK AT AN OLD MEDIUM

Papier-mâché is an age-old medium that has been around since paper was invented in the second century, and it never seems to lose its relevance. Literally translated as "mashed paper," papier-mâché is an extremely accessible medium that appeals to both adults and children. Creations can be as simple or as complicated and as big or as small as you like. If you want to see papier-mâché at its finest, or if you are just seeking some serious inspiration, take a look at the beautiful and innovative Papier-mâché work of contemporary Mexican artists Sergio Bustamante and Felipe Linares Mendoza or U.K. artist Julie Arkell.

Papier-mâché easily captures the spirit of whimsy and, best of all, can be made entirely from recycled materials. Finally, a use for all that junk mail! Depending on what you want to create, papier-mâché sculptures can be worked over or inside a mold or built on top of an armature. Anything that can function as an inner support or framework can be considered an armature, including cardboard, wire, or crumpled papers.

PAPIER-MÂCHÉ PASTE RECIPE

INGREDIENTS

2 cups (250 g) flour (non-self-rising wheat or rice flour) or cornstarch

2 cups (470 ml) boiling water

2 cups (470 ml) cold or room-temperature water on reserve

½ cup (100 g) sugar

several drops of preservative oil (see essential oils guide on page 33)

glue (optional)

INSTRUCTIONS

1. In a large bowl, combine flour, sugar, and boiling water. Mix well.

2. Add the preservative oil of your choice, and allow the mixture to cool and thicken. Look for a yogurt consistency. You can adjust your paste by adding more water from your reserve if the mixture becomes too thick.

NOTE: You'll notice some slight variations in the characters of the different flours. For example, cornstarch generally requires more water, and rice flour needs to more time to thicken.

3. For added strength, add glue to the mix. Any of the adhesives from Chapter 2 will work, but you can use any glue, as long as it is water-based. If you decide to add adhesive, add it while the paste is warm; it will mix better.

4. While your paste is cooling, build your armature or prepare your mold. If your mold is an object such as a bowl or a plate, prepare the surface with a layer of cooking oil, so the papier-mâché can easily be removed when it is dry. Thinking ahead to the final form of your sculpture will help you determine the best way to build the armature.

5. When your papier-mâché paste has cooled to room temperature, you are ready to begin.

PAPIER-MÂCHÉ BIRDS

MATERIALS

paper from the recycling bin, torn into strips

cardboard armature

papier-mâché paste (see recipe on page 56)

optional: flying bird templates to use for armature (page 127)

Almost any paper can be used for papier-mâché: brown bags from the grocery store, junk mail, newspapers, newsprint, old journal or notebook paper, magazines, and computer/copy paper. For a smooth finish, use tissue paper as the final layer—the thinner the paper, the finer the surface.

When preparing your paper pieces for papier-mâché, tear the paper into strips, rather than cutting it with scissors. This allows the paper fibers to fuse more easily during the drying process. Sculptures with lots of little details will require small, thin strips; use bigger strips for large or simple shapes.

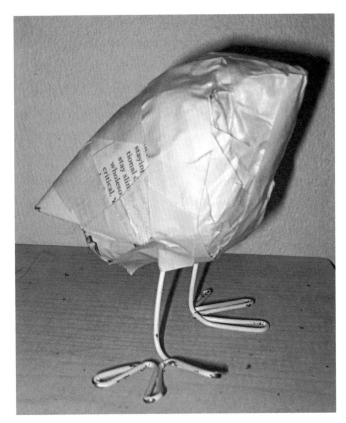

LEFT: String was used to allow this papier-mâché bird to stretch her wings and fly. The bird was painted with milk paints and given a dark patina using india ink. The beautiful yarn was created from colorful recycled silk saris.

TOP: The armature for the body of this little bird was built and shaped with crumpled magazine papers and masking tape. Feet fashioned from an old wire clothes hanger were pushed into the body.

BOTTOM: This bird armature, used for the bird on page 58, was built from cardboard. To join the wings to the body, cut a slit in the body and slide the wings through it.

INSTRUCTIONS

1. Submerge each strip entirely into the papier-mâché paste mixture and remove the excess by running the strips between your fingers.

2. When placing the strips onto your base, overlap and crisscross the strips to give the finished piece added strength.

3. Once you have sufficiently covered your mold or armature with layers of paper, place it in a good spot (preferably with some fresh air and sunshine) and let your new sculpture dry. Rotate the sculpture occasionally during the drying process. Depending on your climate, the drying time can range from a day for dry climates to a week for more humid climates. To be certain that the piece is completely dry, let it sit an extra day or two before painting it.

4. When your sculpture is dry, it's ready to be painted or collaged. Apply a generous coat of gesso or white paint to seal the surface of the dried paste and prime and prepare the sculpture for color.

5. When your primer coat is dry, paint your sculpture with a permanent paint, such as acrylic, latex, or milk paint. If you prefer to collage the surface, use an acrylic medium.

CREATING A DARK PATINA

To give your sculpture an aged look and feel, use india ink (see recipe on page 61). When your paint is completely dry, paint one side completely with the ink. Let it set for about 30 seconds, then wipe off the ink with an old cloth rag. If there is more ink on the surface than you care for, dampen the rag with water and continue wiping until you are satisfied with the finish. Repeat the process on the other side of the sculpture.

SIMPLE INDIA INK RECIPE

India ink, also known as Chinese ink, has been used since the fourth century. The basic recipe for india ink combines carbon black pigment (such as lampblack, made from soot or burned wood), found at specialty art-supply stores that carry dry pigments, with a water-soluble binder, such as gelatin or gum arabic. Mix a small amount of both ingredients, starting with a one to one ratio, in a bowl. Add more binder if you need a smoother, more-fluid flow; add more pigment for a more-opaque ink body.

BELOW: This little papier-mâché bird sculpture was painted with low-VOC latex paints. Because he stands alone and relies on his little feet for stability, adjustable wire hanger pieces were used to give him a secure stance. The purple foil heart, as seen in the photograph on page 57, was created from a foil candy wrapper.

PAPIER-MÂCHÉ PRAYER BEADS

MATERIALS

- paper from the recycling bin
- papier-mâché paste (from recipe on page 56)
- acrylic, latex, or milk paint
- collage paper scraps
- gel pens and/or markers
- bookbinder's awl
- waxed linen

Many cultures and religions have a tradition of using prayer beads to keep a count of prayers, chants, or devotions. The number of beads used in a set of prayer beads usually has a spiritual significance. Buddhists and Hindus generally have 108 beads to represent the 12 astrological zodiac signs multiplied by the 9 planets of our solar system. Episcopal and Protestant rosary bead strings contain 33 beads to represent the 33 years of Jesus' life, and Muslims use 99 beads, which represent the 99 names of Allah. Regardless of your beliefs or faith, creating a set of your own prayer beads can be a powerful tool for centering the creative spirit within. Choose your own personal number of beads according to what you want to empower or represent.

Most papers, from book and copy papers to cardboard, newspaper, and junk mail, will work for this project. This set of prayer beads was created from recycled paper pulp made from old art journal papers and book pages with prayers, dreams, and intentions written on them. Infuse your beads with personal spirit by writing hopes, prayers, or blessings onto your papers before tearing them up to make your beads.

INSTRUCTIONS

CREATING THE BEADS:

1. Prepare your papers by tearing them into tiny bits and squares.
2. Prepare a bowl of warm water and submerge the torn papers into the water. Soak the papers overnight or for about 24 hours to let the paper fibers loosen up.
3. Drain the water out of the bowl and add enough papier-mâché paste to cover all the papers. Be sure to mix the papers and paste together really well. For an extra-fine paper pulp mix, you can mix the papers and paste together in an old blender (do NOT use the family blender for this project!).
4. Prepare a tray or cookie sheet with a sheet of wax paper on which to place and dry your beads.
5. To create a bead, pinch out bits of pulp from the bowl and squeeze out the excess water. Roll the pulp in your palms to form a ball and set it on the tray or cookie sheet to dry. The size and shape of the beads are up to you.
6. Repeat this process until you have created the desired number of beads.
7. Place your beads in a sunny spot with fresh air to dry. As with all papier-mâché projects, drying time is relative to your climate. A day or two should be sufficient, depending on the size of your beads. Large beads may take a bit longer, small beads should dry more quickly.
8. Once the beads are dry, they are ready to be painted, collaged, and embellished.

STRINGING THE BEADS:

1. Strong and easy to thread through an embroidery needle, waxed linen is a good fiber choice. Double up the thread and knot the end, leaving a few extra inches of thread tail.

2. Begin stringing the beads, tying a knot in the thread in between each bead to control the layout of your necklace.

3. Continue until you have threaded the desired number of beads.

4. Finish the necklace by stringing through the very first bead (or through the first few, as seen in this necklace), knot, and adorn the remaining thread tassels.

5. To give the final piece a darker patina, pour some india ink into a lidded plastic container. Place the entire string of beads into the container, close the lid, and shake it up. Remove the excess ink from the beads with a damp cloth rag, and hang the piece in a cool, dry place to dry.

6. When the beads are dry, bless the necklace with your first prayer!

DECORATING THE BEADS:

1. To get the paint on all sides of your beads, put a couple of tablespoons of paint and a couple of teaspoons of water inside an old plastic container.

2. Mix the paint and water together, then sprinkle in a handful of beads. Close the lid and shake them up. Open the lid and check that each bead has been covered completely, repeating the process if necessary.

3. Remove the beads from the container and set them back on the tray or cookie sheet to dry. This process can be repeated with numerous colors; just be sure to let each layer of paint dry well between coats.

4. When the paint is dry, embellish the beads with gel pens and collage-paper scraps. Be sure to use permanent gel pens and markers, so all your hard work does not get wiped away if your beads get wet. An acrylic medium can be used to glue collage papers onto the beads.

5. As the acrylic dries, push holes through the beads using a bookbinder's awl. Be careful not to poke your hands or fingers! If your beads are too thick or too large to push through, a hand drill (such as a Dremel) fitted with a small drill bit can be used to make the holes.

The following Iroquois Prayer of Thanks was (and is still some-times) used at the beginning and end of personal and community events. It is a fitting tribute to the many creatures and elements of the Earth. Use it for inspiration.

We return thanks to our mother,
the Earth, which sustains us.
We return thanks to the rivers and streams
which supply us with water.
We return thanks to all herbs, which furnish medicines
for the cure of our diseases.
We return thanks to the corn, and to her sisters,
the beans and squashes, which give us life.
We return thanks to the bushes and trees,
which provide us with fruit.
We return thanks to the wind,
which, moving the air, has banished diseases.
We return thanks to the Moon and the stars,
which have given us their light when the Sun was gone.
We return thanks to our grandfather Thunder,
that he has protected his grandchildren from witches and reptiles,
and has given us his rain.
We return thanks to the Sun,
that he has looked upon the Earth with a beneficent eye.
Lastly, we return thanks to the Great Spirit,
in whom is embodied all goodness,
and who directs all things for the good of his children.

STRETCHING YOUR OWN CANVAS

MATERIALS

set of stretcher bars (preferably
    from sustainable wood)
canvas
staple gun

OPTIONAL TOOLS:
canvas pliers
canvas hammer
squaring tool

INSTRUCTIONS

1. Attach the stretcher bars together, corner to corner. The tongue-and-groove corner slots of commercial stretcher bars make them easy to assemble. Secure the connections by hand or by tapping the corners tight with a hammer. Use a squaring tool to check that your corners are square.

2. Lay out your canvas and place the assembled stretcher bars on top. Trim the canvas to size, leaving about 4" (10 cm) on each side of the stretcher bars.

TIP:
Save the cut canvas fragments and sew them together to create a unique canvas!

3. Starting with the side closest to you, pull the canvas up over the stretcher bars and add a staple.

4. Rotate the canvas 180 degrees, pull the canvas snug, and add a second staple.

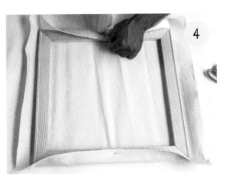

5. Turn the canvas 90 degrees, pull the canvas snug, and add a third staple. Finally, turn the canvas 180 degrees, pull the canvas snug, and add a fourth staple. Check your corners again, to be sure they are still square.

6. Now that your canvas is stapled to all four sides, continue to tighten up and staple the canvas on each side

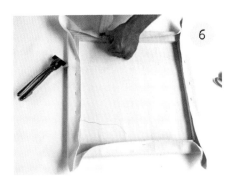

7. Corners can be tricky, because you want them to lay as flat as possible. Pull down the top corner of the fabric and use your thumb to tuck it down into the side of the stretcher bar. Staple down the first fold. Pull the other fold over firmly and add another staple. Add additional staples, if necessary.

Voilà! Your very own stretched canvas. Apply a couple of coats of gesso to the surface and you are ready to paint.

AXIS MVNDI

BOOKMAKING:
NOTEPADS AND JOURNALS
FROM RECYCLED MATERIALS

Going green doesn't mean you have to give up your love of books! Chances are, you have stacks of junk mail, notebooks with empty pages, and even paper remnants from other projects around the house. The altered book movement has taken the stigma out of painting in old books and given new life to discarded or damaged library and thrift books.

The following projects can be put together without a trip to the art-supply store, using materials you already have around the house or studio. You will learn two techniques for creating a cover and how to bind in pages using simple stitches.

·BOOK OF·

INTENTIONS·

REPURPOSING AN OLD NOTEBOOK

MATERIALS

old notebook

paper remnants

fabric

wood paint stirrer or ruler

glue (see recipes, pages 44–47)

waxed linen

acrylic, latex, or milk paint

OPTIONAL MATERIALS:

gel pens or markers

collage paper bits or images

rubber stamps and permanent ink pad

TOOLS

bookbinder's awl or Japanese screw
    punch

embroidery needle

hand drill

When building a book from scratch, start with a strong, solid foundation. For this project, an old composition book with leftover unused pages was dismantled to provide the cover and pages for a new book. If you don't have an old composition book handy, cardboard pieces, canvas panels, heavy stock matte board, or any other heavyweight paper materials you want to recycle can be used in place of the composition book covers and wood spine. Experiment with materials you find around the studio!

INSTRUCTIONS

FOR THE COVERS:

1. Dismantle the book by using a craft knife to cut the stitching in the center of the book. Carefully snip each stitch to make removing the pages easy. Pull out the pages and discard remaining threads.

2. Put the pages aside and separate the front and back covers by cutting the binding down the center of the spine.

3. To create a new spine for the book, cut the wood ruler or paint stirrer to the length of your cover using a craft knife. To do this, mark a cutting line on the front and on the back of the ruler with a pencil, then carefully run the blade over the marks several times. When you have scored both sides several times, you should be able to snap it.

4. Lay the covers and spine onto a piece of fabric (cotton seems to work best, particularly in the gauge of an old sheet or pillowcase) leaving approximately ¼" (6.35 mm) of even space between the spine and each of the covers.

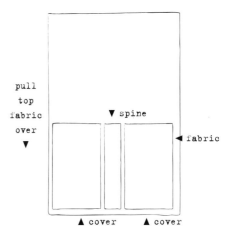

5. Cut the fabric, leaving approximately 1" (2.5 cm) around the sides and bottom of the covers and enough fabric on top to fold down and cover the inside of the notebook.

6. Generously cover the front and back covers and spine with glue and lay back in place on the fabric. Add additional glue to the spaces between the spines and covers and around the edges of the outer fabric.

7. Pull the top fabric over the top of the covers and spine and adhere it to the inside of the covers, making sure to work out any air bubbles with your hands. Flip the covers over and remove any air bubbles on the outside covers and spine. This is your chance to add more glue to any areas that are not adhering well.

8. When everything is glued into place, set your covers aside to dry for a few hours. In the meantime, start prepping the pages.

FOR THE INSIDE PAGES:

1. Using the removed notebook pages as a template, cut additional pages. For this book, Rhimax's Organic Multipurpose Paper, a 100-percent recycled paper in a beautiful brown finish in a nice heavy stock, was used for the additional pages. This paper also works well for covering and protecting your work surface. When you need to change it, recycle the paper into a project.

2. Fold your new pages to match the notebook pages, then nest them inside each other, making two equal-numbered sets of pages (these are called signatures). Set the pages aside.

EMBELLISH THE COVERS:

1. When your covers are almost dry, trim off the excess fabric along the sides and bottom to about ¼" (6.35 mm). This fabric can be decoratively stitched later, or you can trim it down with pinking shears. You can now begin embellishing the covers. For this book, the outside covers were stained with a wash of low-VOC ocher latex paint. To create a paint wash, add enough water to a water-based paint to give it transparency, then brush it over your surface. To give the covers a distressed look, wipe areas while the wash is wet. Add dimension by applying a darker color wash along the edges.

2. To give the cover an additional handmade touch, the main focal image, a digital print, was stitched to the cover with a sewing machine (this can also be done by hand; use a bookbinder's awl to pre-punch your holes). Decorative stitches were also added along the edges of the cover fabric and along the sides of the spine.

3. To make your stamped images pop, paint a light color over the areas onto which you plan to stamp. Further embellishments were made along the edges using gel pens, stamps, and markers.

TO MAKE THE BINDING HOLES:

You don't have to be a mathematician to know where to put the binding holes in the papers and spine.

1. To find the right spot, cut a paper template of your book's spine. Fold the template down the center *lengthwise* and run your nail along the fold to make a sharp edge. Now fold the halves in half again making sharp folds.

2. Open up your folds; your template should be divided into four even sections.

3. Repeat the process by folding the template in half *widthwise*, and those halves in half.

4. Open up your folds; you now have a spine template with a grid for finding and making your holes. Use a pencil to mark the points where the long folds along either side of the center and every other fold along the short folds intersect (see photo on page 75).

5. Using a bookbinder's awl or Japanese screw punch, punch holes into your template at the pencil marks. A Japanese screw punch is an invaluable tool that makes the binding process much easier by punching clean, wide holes through your signatures.

6. Once your book covers are dry, line the punched template over the inside of your spine. Mark the holes onto the spine with a pencil or marker.

7. Remove the template and drill holes into your spine using a hand drill (such as a Dremel) with a small drill bit. The size of your hole is determined by the size of your drill bit, so keep this in mind when choosing your bit. You'll need to be able to fit a threaded embroidery needle through the hole.

8. Using the spine template on 127, line up the punched folds over the center fold of your first signature. Mark the holes with a pen or marker (see illustration below).

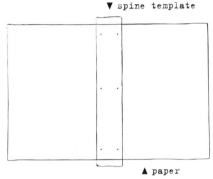

9. Remove the template and punch the holes. Repeat this process with the other signature. To keep the pages from moving, clamp the pages of each open signature together along the edges with a couple of bull clips before you make the holes. Keep the clips on during the sewing process, as well, to help keep the holes aligned.

TO ASSEMBLE THE BOOK:

Now that you have the binding holes in the spine and corresponding holes in your signatures, you are ready to sew your book together. Each signature is sewn in independently to ensure that the finished book is nice and snug.

1. Double-thread your embroidery needle with about two generous arms' lengths of waxed linen. Double-knot the end, leaving a tail of about 2" (5 cm).

2. Starting from the top outside hole of the spine, bring your needle through the spine and sew through the top outside hole of the first signature group of papers (see illustration below).

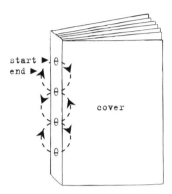

3. Move down to the next hole on the inside of the signature and bring your needle through the papers and out through the corresponding hole in the spine. Move down to the next hole. Repeat this process until you get to the bottom hole.

4. Once you have threaded through the bottom spine and signature hole, make your way back up the book, through the same holes, as per the illustration.

5. When you have reached the second-to-last hole, tug the strings tight and tie them off to the tail of the starter knot. Repeat the process with the second signature.

6. When your signatures have been sewn into place, adorn the strings with beads, if you like, then trim the strings about an ⅛" (3 mm) from the knot.

FUSED PLASTIC BAG LIST-MAKER'S JOURNAL

MATERIALS

plastic shopping bags

wax paper

paper remnants

waxed linen

TOOLS

an old iron

embroidery needle

bookbinder's awl or hand drill

The perfect book for the list-maker on the go, this book is made entirely from recycled materials. When the pages are all full, just remove the binding and add new pages. Recycled shopping bags were used to create the sturdy, fused-plastic cover. A strong, versatile material, homemade fused plastic is being used to make everything from messenger bags to clothing. It's easily obtainable and can also be quite beautiful.

TO FUSE THE PLASTIC BAGS:

1. Begin by cutting your plastic bags into similar-sized sheets. Place a sheet of wax paper onto your worktable and stack the plastic sheets on top. A minimum of 6 sheets provides a good gauge of finished plastic. To create a layered collage effect, insert cutout shapes and text from a variety of colored plastic bags between the sheets. Once your plastic is arranged, top the stack with another sheet of wax paper.

2. With your iron set to medium-high, begin ironing the top sheet of wax paper. Depending on your iron, you might need to adjust your heat settings. Be sure to keep moving the iron around, so the plastic underneath doesn't completely melt.

3. Flip over the entire stack of plastic, including the wax paper sheets, and repeat the ironing process. To test that your plastic is sufficiently fused, see if the sheets pull away from each other. If they pull apart, they need more time under the iron. If they do not pull apart, you are ready to create the journal cover.

4. Remove the wax paper and clean up the page edges by trimming off stray bag fragments.

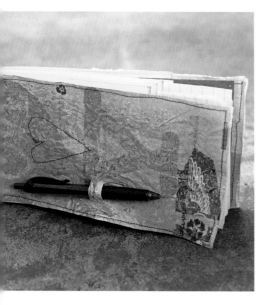

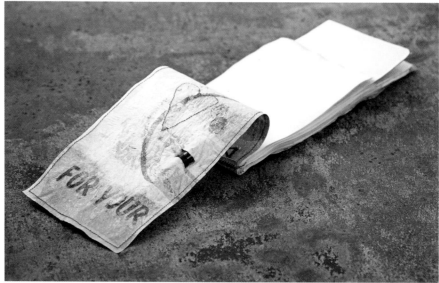

To create the covers:

1. Gather up extra paper scraps, junk mail (blank sides up), and old notebook pages and trim them to the desired page size. You don't necessarily need to fold your pages for this book project, unless you want to vary the paper lengths within the book.

2. Next, size your fused plastic to create front and back covers for the pages. For a neat, clean finish, sew the front and back covers together at the top to create one long sheet, which can be folded over to cover the exposed paper edges. While the covers were on the sewing machine, a decorative stitched edging and a stitched heart were added.

front   ▲ sew   back

3. To punch the holes, stack the paper pages together, making sure that the pages are flush to the top edge. Wrap your book cover around the papers.

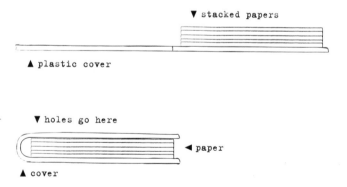

▼ stacked papers

▲ plastic cover

▼ holes go here

◀ paper

▲ cover

4. You don't need to be precise when placing the binding holes. Just be sure to create two rows of four holes, leaving approximately 1" (2.5 cm) between the holes, top to bottom. Place the first set of holes about ¼" to ½" (6.35 mm to 1.25 cm) from the top edge, and leave the same space between the last hole and the bottom edge of the cover.

5. Because this book was made with a thick stack of several types of paper, a hand drill was used to make the binding holes. A Japanese screw punch can also be used, but the job requires a bit more elbow grease.

To assemble the book:

Although any stitching can be used to bind the book, this project was created using a series of cross stitches (see diagram at right). The single line represents the first group of stitching, from left to right; the double lines represent the second group of stitching, from right to left.

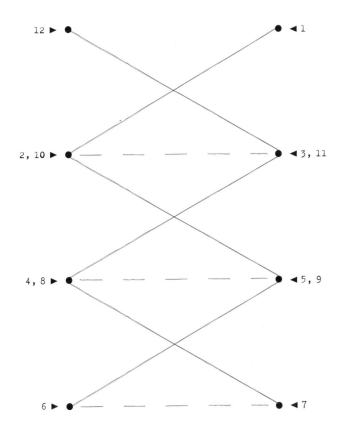

1. Double-thread your embroidery needle with about two generous arms' lengths of waxed linen. Double-knot the end and leave a tail of about 3" (7.5 cm); you will use this tail to tie off the stitches.

2. Starting with the top left hole, come up through the hole from behind (1). Cross down and go through the second hole in the lower column of holes (2).

3. Come straight up and through the second hole in the upper column (3) and down through the next hole in the lower column (4).

4. Come straight up through the third hole in the upper column (5) and down through the last hole in the lower column (6). Because this is the last hole in the lower column, you will now come up through the top right hole of the upper column (7) and, using the same stitching technique, start making your way back across (8, 9, 10, 11) to the bottom left hole (12). You should end up with a series of X's.

5. Go down through the lower left hole, then up to the top left hole (1) and tie the two ends together with a double knot up at hole (1). If you like the look of the stitching in between the X stitches, you can repeat this process starting from the back side.

6. To finish the book, use a craft knife to cut two ¾" (2-cm) incisions, about 1" (2.5 cm) apart, in the cover to hold a pen or pencil. Now pop it into your bag and enjoy!

When the pages are full, simply unstring the binding and stitch in some new sheets.

USING FOUND OBJECTS
IN YOUR ART

Found objects that are repurposed and recycled are perhaps the greenest of materials. You are giving new life to objects that no longer serve their original function and finding new ways to re-incarnate them. Scouring yard sales and thrift stores and digging deep into your drawers and closets can yield fun and interesting objects for shadow boxes and assemblages.

This piece was created with collected findings from the sea and shore as an homage to summertime memories and adventures. A repurposed toy box for the shadow box and a button sample background sheet created a solid base for all the little found gems. The rocks and seashells were added using a hot glue gun, and a combination of watercolors, low-VOC latex paints, and gel pens provided the colors. The cotton ribbon was stiffened with a layer of paint, then stamped and tacked onto the shadow box with a pair of small wire nails. When finished, shadow boxes can be displayed on a shelf or, with the simple addition of a saw tooth hanger, be hung on a wall.

TIP:

When joining parts with adhesive, be sure that the pieces are clean and dry before applying glue. Gently sanding the pieces with fine-grit sandpaper gives the glue a good "tooth" to hold on to.

USING PHOTOS IN YOUR ART

Digital cameras have helped us all become "greener" photographers by eliminating the toxic chemical dependence and restrictions of film and photo processing and allowing us to print from our home computers. Although going digital means we can shoot as many as 500 photos at a time, printing only the photos we choose has also cut back tremendously on waste. Home printers generally use water-based inks, and the ink cartridges can often be refilled or recycled. Even better, many digital cameras come standard with rechargeable batteries, further eliminating waste by keeping used batteries out of landfills.

Digital photography puts an entire image library at your fingertips, making experimentation much more affordable and easier than ever. It also makes it possible to easily share your world with others, by posting your photos to blogs and other photo and social networking sites.

Sometimes, however, the average photo needs a little something extra to pull the viewer in. Photo editing software, such as Adobe Photoshop, provides endless possibilities for altering photographs in creative and unusual ways.

WORKING WITH TEXTURES

Textures can enrich almost any photo by adding dimension and a layered feel to your image surface.

INSTRUCTIONS

TO CREATE A TEXTURE:

This texture was created by altering an old photograph that was processed traditionally at a local camera shop.

1. Place the photo under running water to moisten the emulsion on the surface of the photo.
2. Using fine grit sandpaper, gently sand away the image, starting from the center and working your way out to the edges. Counter your sandpaper strokes to help blend in your marks. If you prefer a rougher look, use a heavier grit sandpaper or make marks with other objects, such as an awl or scissors.
3. Once you have created a texture you are happy with, wipe away the emulsion pulled off by the sandpaper. Dry your photo and scan.

texture

+ image

= final altered photograph

same texture in
black and white

+ image

= final altered photograph

FOR THE FINAL IMAGE:

1. Once your texture is scanned, select the area you would like to use and crop it.

2. Using the marquee tool in the toolbar, select the image and copy it.

3. Open the photo you want to use with the texture. Paste the texture onto your photo. If your texture does not fit within the dimensions of your photo, go to Edit > Transform > Scale in the upper drop-down menu and adjust the size. Press enter or return to set the new size.

4. Right click the texture layer and select Blending Options.

5. Change the Blend Mode drop-down menu from Normal to Overlay. In this area, you can adjust the opacity of the texture, making it as strong as you like. You can also adjust colors by using the RGB check boxes. When you have finished playing around in this area and are satisfied with your results, click OK.

6. Save your new image as a JPG file and share it with your friends!

TIPS:

- Create textures by scribbling and drawing on paper with pencils, charcoals, and pastels. Or place found objects, such as driftwood, leaves, or old book pages, on your scanner bed and scan them.

- Place objects such as coins and keys under your photos before sanding to create interesting and unexpected textured silhouettes.

- You can keep your texture true to color or convert it to black and white by going to Image> Adjustments> Black and White.

JUXTAPOSING DIGITAL IMAGES

Juxtaposing digital images can create, suggest, or express a visual storyline between two images that, individually, would seem to have no connection. A story that conjures emotions and implications can be told with or without the use of words.

INSTRUCTIONS

1. To combine two digital images in Photoshop, open the two images you want to work with. Check the image sizes by going to Image> Image Size in the upper drop-down menu.

2. Once you know the sizes of both photos, create a new file that can hold the two images together by going to File> New and entering the desired dimensions.

3. Copy and paste each image into your new file. Each pasted image will go into its own layer, so to move or adjust the pasted image, click on the Images layer in the layers window.

4. To move the pasted images around, select the move tool in the toolbar window.

5. To adjust your pasted image, go to Edit> Transform and select Scale, Rotate, Skew, Distort, Perspective, or Warp, depending on how you want to adjust the image.

6. To arrange the order of the layers, drag and drop them over one another in the layers window.

7. Save your new image as a JPG file and upload it to your blog or photo-sharing website.

PURSUIT

TIP:
Thrift stores and yard sales are great places to find old frames to recycle and repurpose. Focus on the shape and form of the frame—almost all frames can be repainted to suit your project. Before painting a repurposed frame, wipe it with a damp cloth and add a primer coat of white paint. This will help the paint color you use to "pop" and be true to color.

PAINTING AND SEWING OVER PHOTOS

Chances are, you have boxes full of wonderful old photos of captured moments, objects, places, and people that can be used in your artwork. These can be altered and used as collage backgrounds or cut with die cuts and used as embellishments. When working with your own personal imagery, you infuse your artwork it with a personal story and experience that is unique. Bring that box of photos over to the worktable and see what you come up with! Here are some ideas to get you going.

SEWN PHOTOS

Photo paper has a heavier body than printing paper, so photos hold up to hand- and machine-stitching quite well. This piece started with a close-up photograph of a seashell. It was stitched on a sewing machine, following the spiral composition of the shell, but it could also have been stitched by hand. A vintage upholstery fabric remnant was stitched onto recycled brown background paper, and the photo was sewn on to function as a pocket. A feather collection was inserted into the new pocket, and the piece was placed into a painted thrift frame.

TIP:

Before tossing or giving away your old clothes, examine the fabric and ask yourself whether it could be used in a future art project. Cottons, especially, or anything with handwork on it, such as embroidery or lace, work well. If you feel it might work for you, cut out just the usable parts of the fabric; this will make storage and organization easier.

PAINTED PHOTOS

Using a photo as a base for painting can provide an opportunity to create interesting results, by enhancing parts of the photo or painting out areas you want to hide. Almost any paint can be applied over a photo. Use acrylic, latex, gouache, or milk paint for an opaque finish and watercolor paints for a transparent finish. When you're done painting, embellish your images with markers, pens, pencils, paper scraps, and collage elements. To glue elements to your photos, use any glue or adhesive you would use for collage, such as acrylic medium or any of the glues in the recipe section of this book.

This photo was glued onto a repurposed wooden plaque and then trimmed using a craft knife. The circles were sketched out before painting and the background was filled in using a low-VOC latex paint. The final embellishments were created with markers. Simple yet effective.

Have some old film photographs you don't think are artwork worthy? Think again! Here are some more photo-altering tips for old photographs:

* Wet your photo with water and use a book awl or embroidery needle to write, doodle, and scratch into the surface. This works particularly well on dark photos.

* Wet your photo with water and sand away the edges or undesirable areas of your photo.

* Color your photos with water-soluble markers.

* Cut or tear up your photos and sew them back together, creating different compositions.

* Embroider designs onto the surface of your photo.

* Stamp images onto the photo.

* Journal on your photo surface with gel pens and markers and add them to scrapbooks or art journals.

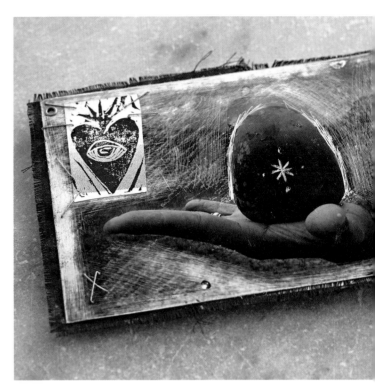

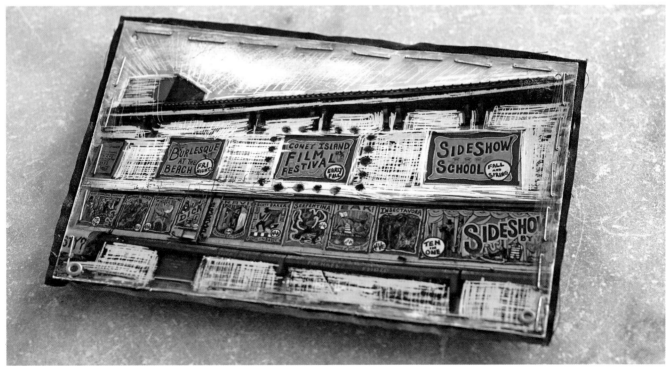

Jane Ingram Allen's larger than life handmade paper sculptures
are beautiful examples of bringing new life to refuse.

THE ARTIST IS A RECEPTACLE FOR EMOTIONS
THAT COME FROM ALL OVER THE PLACE:
FROM THE SKY, FROM THE EARTH, FROM A SCRAP OF PAPER,
FROM A PASSING SHAPE, FROM A SPIDER'S WEB.

-PABLO PICASSO

CHAPTER 4

ARTISTS' GALLERY

For some artists, adopting "green" methods in the studio grows out of an adverse reaction to the industry's traditional materials: headaches induced by oil paint; long-term exposure to toxic metalwork mixtures; worry over what risks their art might pose to their children, and the world.

For other artists, green practices gradually sneak into practice; being green is just as convenient as it is conscientious. Recycling, free-cycling, and trading materials with other artists means not having to buy brand-new "stuff." Collections of this and that grow into a ready-made toolbox, eliminating the need to tap into new resources to create art. The materials are already there, available and ready for new life. Dumpster divers, unite!

Some artists, driven by reading and writing about environmental interests, decide to illustrate their views about this Earth through works that tell a story or connect communities. The purpose or mission of each piece is as important as its visual presentation.

You will see examples of all these kinds of artists here. Each of the artists featured in these gallery pages had a vision of creating, not depleting—of leaving an artistic mark, not a harmful footprint on the earth. They looked at the world around them and decided that their art would preserve and protect, not damage the environment or compromise the health of others. In considering their media and personal enterprises, they made changes in the studio to reflect their interest in sustainability. It's more than an interest, actually. It's a commitment.

Our gallery shares the work of inspiring artists who prove that conscientious crafting is freeing. Deciding to work with the Earth rather than take from it opens up a world of creativity.

INDIA FLINT

BOTANICAL ALCHEMIST

As a cloth colorist, costumer, and designer of r(eco)fashion label "prophet of bloom," a line of hand-sewn, plant-dyed garments, India Flint admits her clothing designs have moved far from mainstream fashion. She describes her wearables as "costumes for living."

Flint's one-of-a-kind fabricated and re-fashioned garments are embellished with stitches, salvaged pearl buttons, and, sometimes, hand-formed wool felt. Flint supplements vintage and second-hand materials with new wool, silk, and hemp—all renewable resources. She experiments with raw materials that she grows (roses, plums, eucalyptus) or finds (wind-fallen leaves, metal scrap) on her 470-acre (190-hectare) Hope Farm in South Australia.

Flint's signature mark is the eucalyptus eco-print. Telling the story behind her adoration for this plant, she recalls collecting hens' eggs one morning on the farm after several days of rain. They were covered with eucalyptus leaf prints. The warm hen's nest and damp leaves caused the shape and color of the soggy foliage to transfer onto the egg "canvas." During that time, Flint was researching more thoroughly the materials she has used for years to dye silk scarves and other garments. She sought alternatives to the dangerous Procion dyes she used during her early training.

Flint began to embrace the traditional fiber-dying techniques of her Latvian maternal grandmother, relying on metals, ash, seawater, whey, and fruit vinegars, among other ingredients to create dyes. She avoids the use of harmful synthetic mordants (chemicals that fix dyes). Every plant bleeds some sort of color in her dye pot, she has discovered. In fact, the same genus and species of plant grown in three different locations can produce three entirely different colors.

"IF THE OBJECTS DON'T FIND HOMES IN THEIR FIRST INCARNATION, THEN I SIMPLY RECONSTRUCT UNTIL THEY DO, WHETHER IN THE FORM OF A GARMENT OR QUILT OR A WALL-CLOTH."

RIGHT: India Flint in "ragged blossom." In this self-portrait, she wears her r(eco)fashion label "prophet of bloom."

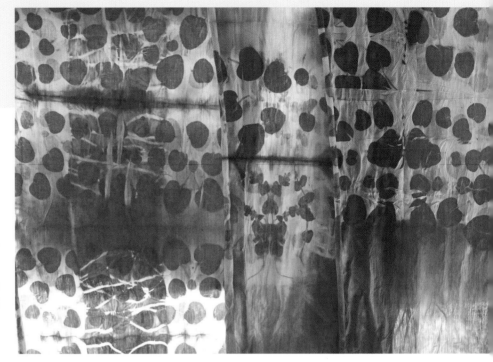

Ecologically sustainable dying with plants doesn't require expensive equipment or a special space. Flint encourages her students to buy dye pots from second hand stores and to collect scrap metals, glass jars, and fallen leaves. To make beautiful ice-flower dyes, Flint harvests frozen purple petals from black violas, stuffs them into a sock, and then soaks the sock in cool water. The result is a brilliant blue dye that colors silk, cotton, linen, and super-fine merino wool.

Plant dyes play in important role in not only embellishing clothing but maintaining them so the garments sustain a longer life. For example, over-dying a wool piece in eucalyptus dye strengthens the fibers and restores the freshness and color of the garment. Flint appreciates wool for the tiny footprint it leaves. It is fire-resistant, responds well to plant dyes, and has antibacterial qualities. It will even biodegrade into the soil if composted.

Flint is the author of *Eco Colour* and co-author of *Hand-made Style: Felt* (both Murdoch Books).

WWW.INDIAFLINT.COM

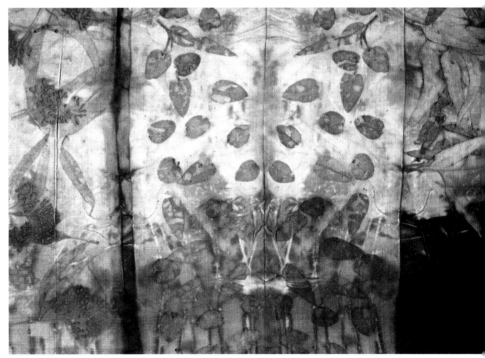

TOP: Eco-print on wool   **BOTTOM:** Eco-print on silk

ABIGAIL DOAN

ART FARMER

GROWING UP IN THE HUDSON VALLEY on a dairy and sheep farm, Abigail Doan was exposed to farming and agricultural practices as a young girl. She traveled to craft fairs with her mother and demonstrated how to spin yarn. Doan's work is rooted in this hands-on, eco-aware foundation, though she shucked what she jokingly calls her Laura Ingalls Wilder youth while attending Purchase College in New York City. There, she worked with traditional materials, such as oil paints, which left her feeling light-headed after hours in the studio. Doan eventually returned to traditional, domestic materials. She preferred pencil drawing and collage using delicate vellum papers and thread-like fiber.

Doan pursued environmental outreach interests. She traveled to India and researched a women's environmental movement there while working on a project with a filmmaker. Her art needed to be mobile, completely portable. And so drawing and collage continued to dominate her portfolio. Meanwhile, the visual aspect of her work as an "art farmer" began to evolve as she took on a activist/documentary role with film and related projects.

The ability to articulate environmental ideas and illustrate them in some art form is a powerful combination for Doan. As an eco-writer and blogger, Doan deposits her ideas about living sustainability in urban and rural environments into the mainstream. Her artwork communicates a harmony between progress and past, modernity and mindfulness. In particular, she creates "mapped and toured textiles" by knotting and twisting found objects from a neighborhood or other designated location into wisps of fiber roving. (Imagine poking wrappers, foliage, and other trinkets you'd find on a walk into a long piece of un-spun wool.) She then hand-spins this urbanized fiber into a piece of fiber art.

Doan titled a project created for New York's 2008 Conflux art and technology festival *Urban Fiber Flotsam*. It was an exploration of how free-floating flotsam, as Doan describes, drifts on the

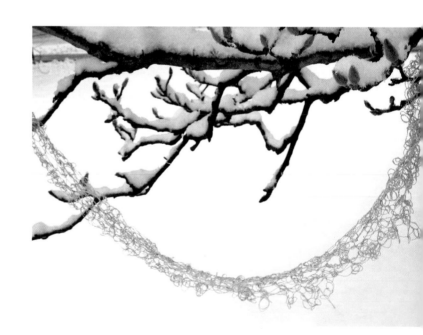

"IN TODAY'S ENVIRONMENTAL ERA, WE NEED TO ADDRESS HOW TO LIVE SUSTAINABLY IN BOTH URBAN AND RURAL SETTINGS."

RIGHT: Crocheted snow is displayed hanging on a branch.

streets and sidewalks. Gathered materials include unanchored litter, random street debris, historical documents, loose vegetation, lost personal artifacts, and culinary ingredients. By collecting and twining these together into a single fiber, Doan aimed to unify the disparate threads of the urban wanderer's experience.

Melding a sense of place into her work is a common theme. Doan splits her time between working from a home studio in New York City and a farm in Tuscany, Italy. She is mother to twins, and her art studio, gallery room, baby toys, and other signs of modern domestic life strewn about her city house serve as inspiration.

ABIGAILDOAN.BLOGSPOT.COM

TIP:

Don't throw away failed projects. Deconstruct them and analyze the pieces and parts. Give yourself time to incubate and discover a solution. Then recycle the items into a new project.

TOP: Groundcover was created using the urban flotsam Doan collected during her city walks.

BOTTOM: Tumbleweed is a handspun concoction of found objects.

LILIAN COOPER

NATURAL FASCINATION

RUGGED LANDSCAPES invite Amsterdam-based artist Lilian Cooper to explore and document. Her naturescape drawings focus on details, such as small fissures, borders and lines, and the subtlest changes, such as the gradual erosion of rock surfaces over time. Paring down these elements, Cooper hones in on her natural subjects to produce abstract drawings using the most basic materials: graphite and pencil, ink, and acrylic paints.

Cooper's work is experiential. She lets the natural world speak to her as she carefully observes the nuances of rugged rocks, mystic elms, coastlines, and woodlands. She spends daylight hours in the field, taking with her a backpack filled with twenty-two pounds (ten kilograms) of drawing equipment and a large roll of paper for sketching. She works without a trace, gathering pencil shavings into containers and taking them home, so she leaves behind no mark.

Cooper is almost halfway through a twenty-year project of drawing rock edges on the North Atlantic coast for her quarry rock series. In her coastline series, Cooper illustrates the edges of the coast, where rock meets sea along the North Atlantic Rim. Trees are a recurring theme in her work. She explores trees and rocks on the edge of a Scottish road, an untamed New England forest, a ruined arboretum of a Devon country house.

Cooper credits her rural English upbringing for her attraction to rocks, trees, the land. She and her Scottish grandmother took walks to look at rocks. Mountains and views represented entertainment—a show. Later, when Cooper studied architecture, the concept of working with and respecting natural materials was reinforced.

"WORKING IN THESE ENVIRONMENTS MAKES ME AWARE OF THE POWER OF OUR NATURAL LANDSCAPES AND FOSTERS A FEELING OF BELONGING TO A BIGGER ENTITY THAT WILL OUTLAST ME."

RIGHT: A twenty-line text installation attached to trees around Weir Farm pond in Connecticut.

While working as an artist in residence in Connecticut, Cooper developed projects that encouraged others to experience nature. For one of Cooper's text pieces, she tagged trees with gardeners' tape labels inscribed with words such as "grow." Nature is art.

"It's a matter of looking intently at the environment and not necessarily taking away materials but perhaps capturing them momentarily in a photograph or drawing, without necessarily touching them," Cooper says.

WWW.LILIANCOOPER.COM

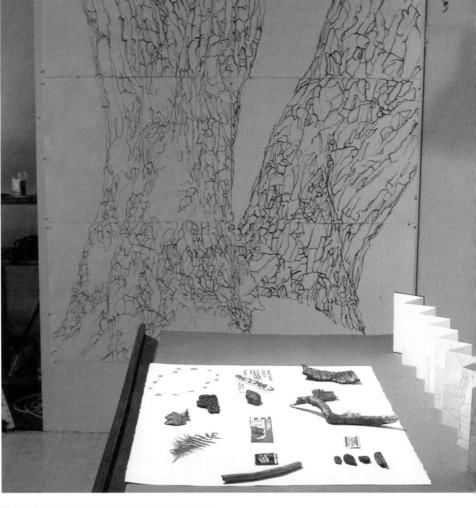

TOP: American Oak

BOTTOM: Drawing a sandstone cliff mural at Les Islomanes symposium in Quebec.

Photographs: Jean-Yves Vigneau

CAT COLLIER

Organic Graffiti

CAT COLLIER CALLS the collection of collaged canvas trees she creates "her forest of thought." Inspired by the vibrantly colored graffiti found on the sides of buildings and bridges and scrawled in the urban landscape, she borrows a similar bold color palette. She scours wallpaper books and has participated in online materials swaps with other artists to build up a stock of papers rich in her favorite colors: teals, emerald, golds, and earth tones.

Collier began focusing on tree collages after hearing a Bible passage from Exodus involving bitter water that the people could not drink, despite their dehydration. As the story goes, the Lord threw a tree branch into the water that sweetened it, so the people could quench their thirst. Collier says the trees' organic shape, their connection to the earth and, in a sense, their soul, inspires her to focus on this subject.

Collier allots only a small budget for her materials because she draws from a collection of vintage wrapping papers left by her grandmother and old wallpaper books she collects from local suppliers. She tapped into the most valuable resource for gathering papers by participating in a handful of online swaps initiated by artist bloggers. Through these, she has gathered old cartoons, a vintage book, fabrics, handmade cards, more wallpaper, and decoupage papers, among other materials. Rather than depleting her most treasured source (her grandmother's wrapping papers), she made color photocopies of these to send to other artists.

Inspiration from magazines such as *Beautiful Decay* and *Juxtapose* provides color theme ideas. Collier will spend a little time doodling, but, for the most part, she takes to the canvas and lets the piece grow as she paints and pastes. Each work gets a dose

of nontoxic Mod Podge adhesive, available in matte or glossy. Lately, she has been cutting out tree trunk shapes from wood-grained contact paper, which adheres nicely to canvas smeared with nontoxic adhesive. An economical approach to purchasing and utilizing materials is important to Collier.

Collier writes about her work at her blog: www.phantom crimes.blogspot.com and is featured in the book *Creative Paper Quilts*, edited by Red Lips 4 Courage and published by Sterling Lark.

TIP:
Collect wallpaper samples and tune into online materials swaps to gather collage materials.

OPPOSITE: Collier's trees—a paper quilt.

TOP: Another work in Collier's "forest" of tree works.

JENNIFER KHOSHBIN

SCULPTURAL STORYTELLER

THE SCULPTURAL BOOK WORKS that Jennifer Khoshbin creates require a tremendous amount of patience and attention. Her canvases are vintage texts—dusty covers forgotten on the back shelves of used book stores. Using a craft knife and other fine cutting tools, she delicately cuts out a silhouette, slicing through each page, one at a time. Hundreds of individual cuttings are required before she, quite literally, digs through the book. The resulting sculpture is then layered with other expressions in paint, pencil, or designer papers.

Khoshbin's *Digging for the Truth* series of small, conceptual pieces began her book project. Inspired by a random exhibit in Philadelphia, she immediately connected to the medium (books) and began to experiment with ways to draw on the inside surface of the book, cutting into the text as a way of delving into the pages and the ideas contained there. Books, Khoshbin says, hold answers to many questions and are an inspiration for creativity. Plus, they are readily available. Khoshbin's home studio contains shelves of used books she has collected—the space looks more like a living room than a workspace, which she prefers.

Khoshbin's *Refarm Spectacle* is a collaborative collection created by Khoshbin and her husband, Paul Lewis, a philosophy professor. They created thirty carved books to "lose" on the sidewalks and alleyways of Houston Street in San Antonio, Texas. The goal was to take the book project to the streets and allow pedestrians to discover, examine, take, or ignore the books. Khoshbin plans to exhaust all of the possibilities of this book project, continuing to devise ways the medium can help explore the world in an interesting way.

Her *Handmade Wilderness* works—papier-mâché wall-mounted deer "trophies"—were born out of the love of animals and inspired by deer art. Fabled stories with animal protagonists are the seeds from which the concept of Khoshbin's *Refarm Spectacle* grew. Khoshbin says the works are "artificially re-imagined." The deer are covered in a variety of designer papers.

Khoshbin comes from a family of artists. Her grandfather was a master carpenter, and so is her uncle. Her mother is a potter, her brother a film artist and curator, and her sister a new-media artist. Khoshbin attended the University of Texas in Austin, where she studied fine arts and sociology, and the University of Kentucky. She is currently restoring a modest 1915 home into a contemporary gallery.

WWW.JENKHOSHBIN.COM

RIGHT: Kitten

TIP:

Be conscious of the products you use. Find out if it's possible to buy in large quantities or to make your own products. Use recycled materials and create a space to work that encourages the thoughtful use of materials, so there is no waste and easy access for recycling. Finally, work on smaller projects, so your artistic footprint is smaller.

" I HAVE MADE A CONSCIOUS DECISION TO WORK SMALLER. I LIKE THE INTIMACY THAT SMALLER WORK CREATES. IT FEELS LIKE AN ALLEGORY FOR BEING CONSCIOUS OF NOT NEEDING TO TAKE UP SO MUCH SPACE IN THE WORLD AT LARGE."

TOP: Butterfly Grave

BOTTOM: Sticks and Stones

JANE INGRAM ALLEN

PLANT-PAPER ARTISAN

JANE INGRAM ALLEN IS IN TAIWAN collecting stray mulberry tree branches and day-lily leaves. Community members help her harvest found foliage, such as leaf droppings and twigs from trees that require pruning anyway. She strips the bark and compiles the leaves into ingredients suitable for producing strong but fine Asian papers, perhaps with sophisticated deckled edges. The paper Allen makes is site-specific. By hand, she labors through the boiling, mixing, beating to a pulp, blending, dipping, and drying steps. The result is an exquisite and strong handmade paper for Allen's mixed-media works, sculpture installations, and site maps.

Allen, who was professor of art for many years, was drawn to from-scratch papermaking art because of its connection to a place and time. Paper is like clay, she says, in that the medium is flexible. You can use it traditionally in flat sheets or weave and knit it with other materials, such as bamboo. (Consider the paper-and-bamboo lanterns commonly found in Asia.) In many ways, papermaking is a scientific type of cooking.

Because creating paper art requires high-quality raw materials (the paper), Allen appreciates the ability to control the process from the very beginning, by choosing plants whose cellulose and fiber will press into a tight mat. Even the same plant collected during different seasons or found in varying soil conditions produces paper with individual colors, textures, and overall properties. That is one of the attractions of making paper from scratch.

As a Fulbright Scholar working in Taiwan, Allen extended her stay there in 2005 with sponsorship from the Taiwan Council for Cultural Affairs/National Endowment for Cultural Art. She visited fourteen different countries while there, collecting plants to make paper and site maps and teaching papermaking workshops to the people. Although Taiwan is a small island, its various ecological regions—high mountains, coastal plains, subtropical, and tropical—offer a variety of plants, and probably the best in the world for papermaking is the mulberry tree, Allen says. Its berries are used for jelly or wine, and birds like to munch on the

"IT TAKES REAL DEDICATION WHEN YOU MAKE PAPER FROM PLANTS. FOR MY WORK, IT SEEMS THE LOGICAL THING TO DO BECAUSE I WANT MY PAPER TO BE VERY SITE SPECIFIC, I ENJOY THE PROCESS, AND IT'S A GREAT ACTIVITY TO DO AS A GROUP."

RIGHT: Ingram Allen beating natural pulp

scarlet fruit. She prefers to use the bark, the strongest part of the tree. It produces a fiber that is sometimes so tough it must be liquefied in a kitchen blender, even after it has been beaten to a pulp.

Allen travels with her work and totes with her a single wooden mallet for beating the paper pulp. She usually connects with local craftspeople to help her make more mallets. She sources pots for cooking and other rudimentary supplies once she is on site. This is another way in which communities participate in her work and learn about her art.

Allen's process has resulted in paper artwork exhibitions in galleries across the world. Her outdoor installations using handmade paper are in public parks, sculpture gardens, and in public buildings and plazas. Allen's work has landed her artist-in-residence positions in Philippines, Japan, Nepal, and Brazil, but she always returns to Taiwan and has spent longer there than anywhere else.

Allen is an art critic and writer for *SCULPTURE* magazine and other art publications.

WWW.JANEINGRAMALLEN.COM

BOTTOM: Made in Taiwan

TIP:
Papermaking has a reputation for being bad for the environment, Allen says, referring to the paper industry's chemical refuse, which seeps into river systems. But there are environmentally friendly ways to make paper. If you want to make paper by scratch, you can trim a plant and really promote its growth—every gardener does that. You can collect dropped foliage. You don't have to cut down a tree.

SUSAN LENART KAZMER

MINDFUL METALWORK

REAL LIFE, STREET LIFE, CITY LIFE, DAILY LIFE: Susan Lenart Kazmer infuses the energy of these experiences and a passion for found objects in her metalwork art and jewelry. A jeweler for twenty-five years, Kazmer once provided wholesale orders—smaller pieces—to Nordstrom, Banana Republic, and Ann Taylor. But she began to analyze whether she wanted to continue putting "stuff" into the world, resulting in a shift of focus to larger pieces with positive content that people can connect with spiritually.

Kazmer is known for mastering cold-join attachments. Beyond the traditional rivet, she'll use fiber-related attachments—such as stitching, weaving, and crochet—and trapeze attachments for objects that require swing and movement. These techniques are outlined in her book, *Making Connections: A Handbook of Cold Joins for Jewelers and Mixed-Media Artists* (2008) and available through her website: www.susanlenartkazmer.net.

Kazmer focuses on ways she can recycle objects and give them new purpose in her work. She'll pick up a piece, perhaps the striker of a typewriter key. She'll hold it, contemplate it, consider its form and possibilities. In fact, typewriter strikers make handy appendages for the delicate metal ballerinas in her Circus Troupe collection. Other useful gadgets Kazmer employs include calculator parts, pencil stubs, jacks, bullet casings, ribbon, handwritten papers, locks, and keys.

The challenge metal artists face is how to pursue their craft in a healthy manner. Polyurethane glues emit a noxious odor that, when inhaled for long periods of time, left Kazmer and her students feeling sick. Plastic, when it is liquid, off-gasses harmful fumes that are detrimental to one's health. Also, after years of soldering and not wearing a mask, Kazmer suffered from heavy copper buildup in her body. She was able to rid herself of the contaminant, but she knows other artisans who became allergic to their medium after mastering it. Most importantly, Kazmer did not want to expose her young children at home to the harmful fumes and other byproducts of her craft.

She began to experiment with ingredients in her kitchen. Partnering with a chemist, Kazmer developed an epoxy resin called "ice resin." The product is nonflammable, contains no solvents, and its worst characteristic is that it causes some people to develop a skin rash. (Use a barrier cream or gloves to prevent this.) Ice resin is compatible with virtually any surface, including many plastics. It can be dyed with craft pigments and used for embedding objects.

LEFT: Bulb necklace

Kazmer uses her ice resin on journal covers to make papers transparent. She "builds" rings out of paper layers, stacking and securing them with the thick epoxy. Because the ice resin squeezes out of its container like a raindrop and stays on a page, she has more control over the product.

Kazmer's latest introduction is her Circus Troupe series (pictured is *The Opera Singer*). The series of figures can be deconstructed into their rings, bracelets, and basic components and worn as jewelry. Together, the materials form a cast of vaudeville-inspired characters that make a statement.

> "I FIND THAT I'M HEALTHIER, BRIGHTER, AND MORE CREATIVE IF I CAN JUST KEEP A SIMPLER LIFESTYLE USING SIMPLER PRODUCTS."

RIGHT: The Opera Singer

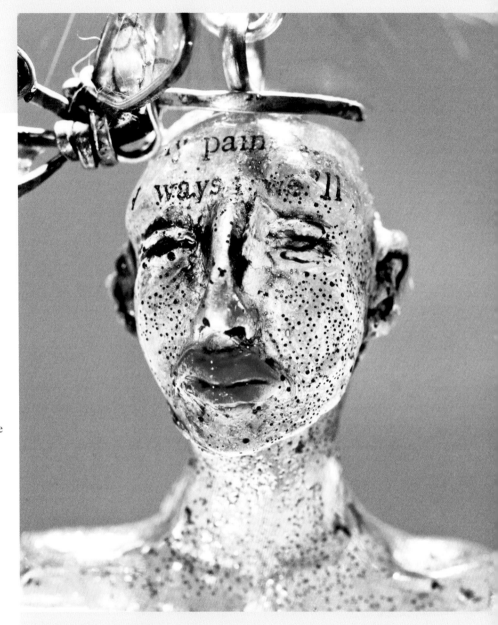

TIP:
Seek out nontoxic resin products and always wear a mask when soldering metal. Find Kazmer's ice resin at www.objectsandelements.com/shop.

BRYANT HOLSENBECK

WASTE STREAM AWARENESS

VISITING A LANDFILL IN Chapel Hill, North Carolina, environmental artist Bryant Holsenbeck's friend, the owner of the site, announced to her, "Welcome to 'away.'"

Throwing away an object doesn't mean it disappears; the environmental responsibility doesn't end once an item is deemed trash and removed from the home. The mindset that our old things "go away" explains why Americans create more garbage per capita than any other culture, Holsenbeck says.

Holsenbeck aims to show communities the sheer volume of material that one can collect over time and how these objects can be reincarnated and transformed into a cultural expression. She collects everyday items such as bottle caps and shoes. She stockpiled mail one year, plastic silverware another year. She has more than 100,000 caps by now, many of them from water and pop bottles. From these, she creates colorful mandalas with the help of schoolchildren or other audiences, who then learn how big the landfill hole must be to contain all that "stuff."

A shoe project Holsenbeck has led with several schools involves asking students to bring to the classroom an old pair of footwear. The children decorate the sneakers with paint and markers, writing down their thoughts on community. Holsenbeck always tells the group, "If you find a pair you want in the pile, they're yours." Many of the children who invest their creative energy embellishing the shoes for the installation want to keep them after the project is over, she says. The children form a winding labyrinth with the shoes. The final product is called *What Do Kids Care About? A Labyrinth of Shoes with Souls Attached*.

Holsenbeck collects materials from friends who set aside bottle caps, plastic bags, or the collection du jour, and leave the bagged items on her front porch. She admits the collections tend to overwhelm her space. She uses a shed behind her home for shoe storage, and bins of caps sit stacked on her screened-in front porch. Her working caps are carefully sorted by color, organized, and ready for use.

"MY MISSION AS AN ARTIST IS TO PROCESS THE STUFF THAT MOST PEOPLE THINK JUST GOES 'AWAY.'"

RIGHT: Holsenbeck and her crows

Holsenbeck's sociology background is a foundation for many of the awareness messages she communicates through her artwork. "I'm looking at the world," she says simply. She began her arts career as a basket maker, then evolved into an environmental artist documenting the waste stream of our society. Art is a way to process life, she says.

Holsenbeck's installation, *Wild Life*, is an attempt to cumulate her thoughts on what she has seen—she wanted to create her own wild space for animals. To do so, she relied on a palette of recycled materials from everyday life. Her investigation is ongoing. Holsenbeck created what she terms a "wild space," using garden hoses, pencils, discarded catalog cards from the University of North Carolina library, ticket stubs, yarn, rubber bands, and other odds and ends. From these items, she fashions birds, snakes, butterflies, and other beasts that inhabit the installations. (Pictured are Holsenbeck and her crows.)

WWW.BRYANTHOLSENBECK.COM

TOP: Bottle cap mandala

BOTTOM: A bird made from recycled, cut-up credit cards

Big Ideas from Little Looms

While haunting a thrift store, Jana Trent ran across a plastic bag holding a pink plastic Weave-It loom. The hand-held craft tool served a utilitarian purpose during the Depression, when several manufacturers produced the 4- and 7-inch (10- and 18-cm) square grid gadgets. Scrap yarn or fabrics woven along the mini-loom pins eventually produced a textile square, which could be used to make clothing or a quilt—or as potholders, washcloths, and other household items. The little looms were ideal for reusing fibers from old sweaters, blankets, or other fabric pieces. People didn't just go out and buy brand-new things in the 1930s.

While examining the found Weave-It loom, Trent, a long-time sewer and home crafter, recalled an article she had read in *Spin Off* magazine that featured a cardigan project assembled from 2-inch (5-cm) woven squares that were dyer samples. She decided the toy-like tool could mimic the project.

Trent began collecting hand-held Weave-It looms. She found them on eBay and in second-hand stores. The simple gadget amused her, and the work she created from the basic tool began to evolve into experimental, inventive projects. She can tap into her creative self when using simpler tools, she says. Without complex equipment, instruction booklets, time spent tinkering with this or that, Trent can focus on imaginative designs. (She still has the complex equipment, she admits: knitting machines, a full-size loom, a sewing machine.)

Trent wants artists to know that the Weave-It is not a novelty. It's a serious fiber tool. "I'm trying to egg people on," she says, hoping crafters will realize the possibilities such a simple tool can offer. Her website, www.eloomanation.com, does just that and also provides free vintage Weave-It patterns.

Trent produces a variety of fabric squares on her Weave-It looms from yarn scrap, vibrantly colored shopping bags she collects (she has a stash her mother saved for years), and materials such as paper raffia, wire, and Himalaya Aloo. Trent uses the squares as embellishments, such as a pocket on a knitted jacket, or she might create a cushion (pictured) from woven plastic bags. She plays with texture and says her projects grow into unique expressions when she uses the materials and tools around her, as opposed to buying new.

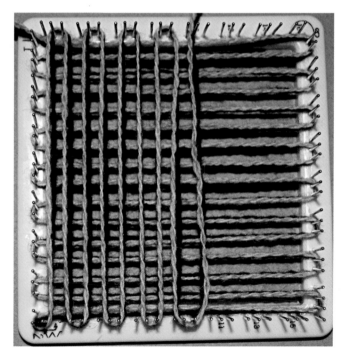

ABOVE: The Weave-It loom

Another plus to using little looms is their portability. Trent can work on projects during car rides, in waiting rooms, and anywhere in her Colleyville, Texas, house.

"THE PRODUCT CREATED FROM A SMALL LOOM IS SO VERSATILE THAT YOU CAN MIX IT WITH ANY OTHER FIBER ART."

TIP:

Search eBay and second-hand stores for basic, even old-fashioned, tools such as the Weave-It loom. Concerning materials, make do with what you have. When you are forced to use what's around you and scale back, you can actually add more interest to a project, Trent says.

RIGHT: A tote made from woven plastic shopping bags

MONICA RIFFE

RECYCLED HEART-FORMS

THERE'S NO SHAME in Dumpster diving. Especially when it wins you several large, black garbage bags full of metal and tin, some still shiny and others rusty or coated with patina. These materials will eventually be sorted and make their way into Monica Riffe's "rin-tin-tin" storage box, in which she keeps a stash of material for her metalwork projects. Riffe has discovered that her daily bike rides are also quite productive, particularly when she finds shelves or wood scrap, furniture, and other household refuse that she can refashion in some way.

Lately, that way seems to be by metalsmithing hearts. (Her twenty-year-old son calls them "vicious hearts," but Riffe explains that's because these hearts are "deeper" than the flat paper cut-outs we're used to seeing around Valentine's Day.) She'll start with a slender pinewood platform, which will readily accept nails if the piece is knot-free. She builds the heart of metal using basic tin snips, a hammer, and nails—the only material she really needs to buy. She adds buttons and upholstery tacks and wooden nickels and Cracker Jack charms. Boxes of tchotchkes provide plenty of options. (Riffe is a saver.) She leans toward purple and red colors,

including terra cotta. Riffe pushes some of the heart designs by incorporating grids and textures into the works. She also combines metalsmithing and tin work by treating patina scrap as the "jewel" in earrings or other pieces.

Riffe, a trained potter, gravitated toward graphic artwork and commercial imagery stamping during the heyday of Uptown Urban Stamp in Fort Collins, Colorado, a hub for artists in the region, she says. Riffe began to design stamps, notably a box set called Shrine of the Divine, with borders and imagery to create a little shrine. She began creating artwork for catalogs and participated in significant collaborative journaling projects with artists such as Lynne Perrella and Nina Bagley (see page 112). Riffe's work is published in seven books, including *Colors: A Palette of Collaborative Art Journals* (Somerset Studio) and *Alphabetica* (Quarry Books).

TIP:

A broken mug without its handle is a handy home for an athletic-sock wipe-up sponge. "I can't live without that little white sock," Riffe says. She first used this method for cleaning rubber stamps.

TIP:

Keep a magnetized nail puller on hand to clean up stray metal shards in your work area. Touch the nail puller to a tiny sliver of metal to pick it up, then tap the metal into the trash. Using the nail puller means you don't have to worry about getting tiny metal pieces stuck in your fingers.

OPPOSITE: A piece from Riffe's heart collection.

NINA BAGLEY

NARRATIVE JEWELRY

NINA BAGLEY KEEPS a small sackful of cut-out words, some from *Reader's Digest* condensed books (she can't figure out why you would *condense* a book), others from old dictionaries and finds from her library's used-book store. The collection becomes a sort of Magnetic Poetry kit.

She instructs her students to reach into the plastic baggie and randomly take out a few words. "What do you see?" she asks them. "What triggers in your head?" The idea is to celebrate the union of word, imagery, and soul.

Found objects such as buttons, beach glass, antique lace, and ribbon help narrate thoughts provoked by the words Bagley clips and saves—or creates by handwriting on treated papers. Bagley will incorporate a word such as "story" by printing it onto coffee-stained paper. Pictured here, the talisman dangles from an eclectic "chain" she created by linking together a 1945 friendship bracelet she found in Wisconsin during travels, a silver postcard charm, and the arm of a tiny German porcelain doll.

Bagley makes "narrative jewelry." Each piece tells the beginning of a different story. It's up to the person wearing or looking at the piece to determine how the tale plays out.

Knickknacks and baubles, heirlooms, and even old magazines provide inspiration and raw materials for Bagley's jewelry. She stores trinkets in antique chests of drawers and vintage tool chests in her 1920s North Carolina mountain home. Beads, ribbon, a drill press, and metal cutter are all close by. Her L-shaped studio, which faces north and east, was too dark inside because

"I DON'T LIKE STAGNANT JEWELRY. I REALLY LIKE PIECES THAT SPEAK TO THE PERSON WEARING IT AND SPEAK TO THE PERSON LOOKING AT IT. FOR JEWELRY TO SPEAK, THERE HAS TO BE A STORY GOING ON. THAT IS WHAT I DO."

RIGHT: Found objects are the basis of Bagley's work. Pictured, "Woodlands Doll necklace"

the sun crawls slowly over the mountain, taking time before morning rays light up the studio. So Bagley clipped fallen tree branches, rigged them with white lights, and fixed them to the walls of her studio to create a cozy wonderland in which she tucks herself away to create her word-smithed jewelry.

Bagley's jewelry design career started eighteen years ago, and she is featured in the book *True Colors: A Palette of Collaborative Art Journals* (Somerset Studio). She has been a guest artist in several books published by Quarry Books.

WWW.ORNAMENTAL.TYPEPAD.COM

TOP: Necklace, entitled "I look back upon our story"

BOTTOM: Tray of Bagley's narrative jewelry

LAUREN FERGUSON

SAFE SOLUTIONS

THE DISPOSAL INSTRUCTIONS for the ferric chloride solution Lauren Ferguson used for etching copper were shocking. (Think blue hazardous waste container, highly toxic.) Ferguson, a mixed-media artist with three young children and a home studio, learned that her son was chemically sensitive to the fumes. What's more, obtaining ferric chloride had become the equivalent of making an arms deal since the Department of Homeland Security added it to a list of chemicals that would no longer be sold to the public. (Think terrorist "orange alert.")

Necessity became the mother of invention for Ferguson.

Her loves are book art and copper etching—fusing these concepts together to create remarkable covers for blank journals. Ferguson is an epidemiologist with a PhD from the Harvard School of Public Health. She was also a librarian, toting a degree from Rutgers. Making books is a natural fit for Ferguson, who purposely leaves the inside pages free of words, like a blank canvas. She lets the copper-etched covers inspire people to fill the pages with their own creations, whether words, collage, or photographs.

When ferric chloride became difficult to obtain, Ferguson decided to do some experimenting. One day, she filled a pink hospital bucket of boiling-hot water with kosher salt, until the water would accept no more. She then used a constant CD current to ionize the saturated saline solution, using a car battery charger, with two copper wires attached to red and black leads, to do the job. After about ten minutes, the copper she exposed to the solution became etched. Ferguson had developed a patent-pending product.

"NECESSITY WAS THE MOTHER OF INVENTION. I BEGAN EXPERIMENTING WITH DIFFERENT WAYS TO GET A GOOD ETCH ON COPPER IN A WAY THAT WAS TRULY GREEN."

RIGHT: Etched copper wall hanging

Needing a way to bottle the solution, she developed what she refers to as "potion A" and "potion B" (the recipe is secret until her patent is approved). When potions A and B are mixed, the chemical reaction allows her to etch copper. She can bottle the AB substance and safely store it—it's not toxic. She can use it again, or she can dispose of it by adding a "potion C," which neutralizes the AB formula. Once neutralized, the solution can be poured down the drain or flushed down the toilet. Stay tuned for more information on the product at www .everythingaltered.com.

Ferguson says there are no mistakes in art—just opportunities. In her case, the result of experimentation is an eco-friendly solution she can use to create her work and leave a lighter footprint.

RIGHT: Copper wire hanging detail

DEEDRA LUDWIG

ARCHIVING NATURE

DEEDRA LUDWIG INVITES her travel experiences into the studio, where she works with nontraditional materials gathered from diverse worldwide locations. Her canvasses serve as calendars or journals, with a "sense of place" embedded and preserved on every surface. Soil, pollen, tree bark, and other organic matter she collects transform into abstract, atmospheric paintings. Each is a visual record of a particular location's evolving naturescape.

Preserving the natural world is important to Ludwig, who works from an urban studio in an old factory warehouse in New Orleans. She has witnessed many dwindling and endangered landscapes, and she tells these evolutionary stories in her works by incorporating the very soil and plant material she finds at a site. The detritus (organic matter of all sorts) she picks up along her journeys is shipped back to her studio in labeled transparent containers. Ludwig has twenty-six years' worth of botanical specimens and soil collected from countries all over the world.

Ludwig says her work shifts and adapts to the changing landscapes she discovers while on residencies in places including the Spanish Pyrenees at the Center for Art and Nature in Farerra, the Cooper Union School of Art and Design in New York City, and the Big Cypress Preserve in Ochopee, Florida, among others. For example, while working in Big Cypress Preserve, she found an ecosystem teeming with species as the season transformed from winter to spring. She happened upon an orchid that was more than 200 years old. These discoveries now show up as subjects and materials used in her body of work.

Natural materials provide fantastic media for painting, Ludwig says. Soil can be ground with a mortar and pestle until it is a fine-textured powder. Ludwig blends the powder with linseed oil until it forms a rich pigment, which she uses with an encaustic mixture. She also uses soil and binder directly on paper and canvas. Many of her pigments include gold leaf, and her work is best viewed in low light, she adds.

Maintaining a safe, nontoxic studio is important. Ludwig will not use formaldehyde-treated wood for canvas stretcher bars, and she uses organic cotton canvas. She recommends seeking out pigments that do not contain VOCs and using proper air ventilation for a healthier workspace. Ludwig gravitates toward natural pigments that are safe and also tell the story of her travels, communicating themes of the ever-changing nature and botanical cycles of growth, death, and regeneration.

WWW.DEEDRALUDWIG.COM

TIP:
Choose materials wisely and support alternative, healthy products. Our work can be both archival and produced with a low carbon footprint.

OPPOSITE: Alchemy and Nature

JUDE HILL

STORY CLOTH

JUDE HILL'S TRAINING as a children's book illustrator is evident in the stories she weaves by criss-crossing fabric scraps she has collected from all over the world and saved during her years spent working in textile design and sales. The quilts she makes are called story cloths. Each work tells a multifaceted tale, one of respect for the cloth and its usefulness and reusability. With every project, Hill tunes into the way the cloth is assembled, its elasticity, thread-count, or texture. All of these nuances add emotion to the finished work. Because each of Hill's story cloths are gifts, the story is very much about the person receiving the cloth (often unknowingly) and Hill's relationship or involvement with that person.

Hill is a saver, a fixer. She doesn't throw out an appliance that doesn't work or toss fabric scraps from her stash if she can find a purposeful afterlife for them. She doesn't go out and buy new "stuff." Hill also makes a conscious effort to use less electricity; she doesn't like noise. These lifestyle decisions are reflected in her artistic process and materials.

Hill recalls a gift she assembled for a friend who built a tree house (for adults) on an upstate New York property. Hill's son helped to build the house, and Hill watched the progress via her friend's blog. She admired the concept of the tree house and her friend's organic lifestyle and commitment to whole living. Hill was also intrigued by the idea of living in a forest, basing the story cloth for her friend on a poem about returning to the forest while we still can. The tree-house quilt was constructed as a housewarming gift without Hill's friend knowing. Hill used no machinery and few stitches, making a "green" quilt that reflected a sustainable lifestyle.

To assemble her cloth stories, Hill begins by collecting scraps of torn-up and/or discarded fabric. Larger pieces might be cut into long, thin strips. Shorter scraps are knotted together. Hill doesn't focus so much on the fabric pattern—no matter if the cloth is stamped with polka dots or a floral print. The integrity of the fabric is most important. Hill lays the strips vertically on her floor and weaves in horizontal strips, much like one would make a little

"I LOVED FIBER SO MUCH, I ACQUIRED A TREMENDOUS COLLECTION OF TINY PIECES OF FABRIC FROM ALL OVER THE WORLD. I BEGAN TO SEW THEM INTO STORIES, WHICH IS MY ART FORM. THAT COMES FROM MY WISH TO TELL STORIES AS A CHILDREN'S BOOK ILLUSTRATOR."

TIP:

"Freecycling" is an important way for Hill to collect materials and involve others in her work. Through the blog community, people have learned about her work on www.spiritcloth .typepad.com. They send Hill free materials, which allows her to incorporate new-to-her fabrics in her quilts and, inadvertently, include the sender in her work.

potholder. She uses no machinery and few stitches, relying on the interlocking pattern and knotting, if necessary, to secure cloth.

Because there is no glue or excessive stitching involved in Hill's process, the result is a soft quilt. (And absolutely no electricity is required.) Her story cloths have a nice drape and often vibrant color themes, as the collection of fabric strips Hill chooses collide into a surprisingly unified work. Hill says her projects are quite portable. She does the piecing together at home and adds detail during her two-hour train rides from her home in Centerport on Long Island to New York City, where she works full-time in the textile business.

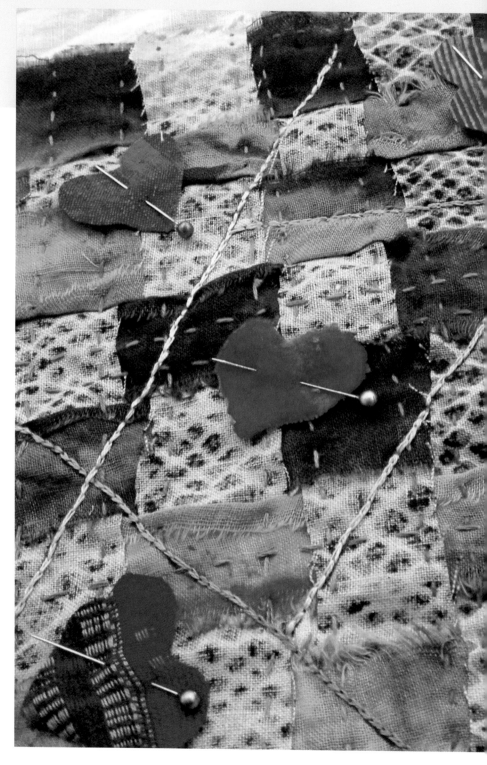

RIGHT: Jude Hill's "story cloth"

BASIA IRLAND

ART AS ACTIVISM

A REVERENCE FOR WATER and its ability to transform life inspires the work of Basia Irland, a sculptor, installation artist, author, and activist who has dedicated her work to celebrating water on a grass-roots level and to raising awareness about the plight of the world's waterways.

Irland is passionate about projects that get her to the river. There, she can communicate visually the importance of preserving our waterways. Irland's works show how rivers are like arteries, connecting communities and serving as the lifeblood of people who gravitate, like her, toward the water.

In particular, Irland has designed numerous Gathering of Waters projects around the country and the world. A canteen and log book become communication tools for diverse people living along a given river. A canteen is passed down the river by hand, and each recipient puts a small amount of water into the container, logging his or her connection or history with the river in the book. Each person who gathers water for the canteen must deliver it downstream to another person, perhaps in another community. The story gradually unfolds.

Along the Rio Grande, the Gathering of Waters exchange occurred for 1,875 miles (3,018 km), from the upper to lower basin. At the close of the project, people traveled miles, and across state lines, to meet and celebrate their connection. One park ranger in Texas had never met a tribe that lived a half-hour down the river. Now they are working together to build a walkway along a portion of the river that connects the dam where the park ranger works and the tribe's community.

Experience and sharing *is* the art of Irland's Gathering of Waters projects. Her purpose is to collect a record of ideas and to pay tribute to the water, always circling back to the theme of reverence for nature.

"A BIG PART OF MY GREEN PRACTICE IS RAISING AWARENESS AND HELPING PEOPLE FIND HEALTHY SOLUTIONS."

RIGHT: Book XVI (French lavender): Arles, France; book placed into an irrigation ditch

Recently, Irland created a series of carved ice books, some weighing 250 pounds (115 kg), embedded with riparian seeds. *Receding/reseeding* emphasizes the necessity of communal effort and scientific knowledge to deal with the complex issues of climate disruption. For some of these carved ice books, water is gathered by participants from a local river, added to a canteen, and handed to others, who decant the water and collect more from the creek in their parts. This ceremony illuminates the point that we all live downstream. The gathered river water is then frozen, carved into the form of an open or closed book, and placed back into the creek. The closed books have seed patterns on the covers. Embedded in rows in the ice of the open books is an "ecological language" or riparian "text," consisting of local native seeds, which are released as the ice melts into the current. When the plants regenerate and grow along the bank, they will help capture carbon and prevent erosion.

The type of seeds she embeds are determined by a region's needs. She has planted ice sculptures with seeds of lavender (Arles, France), olive and wild fennel (northern Spain), and maple (in Paris, France). These ice sculptures completely melt back into nature, leaving behind a beneficial gift: new life.

Irland is based in Albuquerque, New Mexico, and is the author of *Water Library* (University of New Mexico Press). Her prolific career focuses on creating works that share the themes of journey, navigation, and orientation.

WWW.UNM.EDU/~BASIA/BIRLAND

RIGHT: Book XVII (Spanish broom seeds) and Book XVIII (wild fennel seeds): Northern Spain; books placed into the river with Dutch friends, artist Be Van der Heide and Hans Diemal.

ABOVE: Book I (mountain maple, columbine flower, and blue spruce seeds): 250-pound (115-kg) ice sculpture; floated into the Boulder Creek, Colorado.

RESOURCES

GREEN ART SUPPLIES

PAINT

BIOSHIELD NATURAL PAINTS
www.bioshieldpaint.com

DANIEL SMITH
www.danielsmith.com

EARTHPAINT
www.earthpaint.net

EARTH PIGMENTS
www.earthpigments.com

NATURAL PIGMENTS
www.naturalpigments.com

NUTSHELL NATURAL PAINTS
www.nutshellpaints.co.uk

THE OLD FASHIONED MILK PAINT CO., INC.
www.milkpaint.com

THE REAL MILK PAINT COMPANY
www.realmilkpaint.com

SHIVA CASEIN PAINTS
www.artsupply.com

SINOPIA/KREMER PIGMENTS
www.sinopia.com

ADHESIVES AND BINDERS

COCCOINA GLUE STICKS AND PASTE
www.onehundredwishes.com

ECOGLUE, ECOGLUE PREMIUM WOOD ADHESIVE, ECOGLUE EXTREME
www.eclecticproducts.com/ecoglue

METHYL CELLULOSE
www.dickblick.com
www.chemistrystore.com

ORGANIC GELATIN
www.gobiofood.com

ORGANIC GUM ARABIC
www.naturesflavors.com

WELDBOND ALL PURPOSE GLUE
www.dickblick.com
Most craft stores

PAPER

ECO CHOICES
Hemp paper sketchbooks
www.ecoartworks.com

ECOPAPER
Tree-free paper products
www.ecopaper.com

THE GREAT ELEPHANT POO POO PAPER COMPANY
The name says it all!
www.poopoopaper.com

GREEN FIELD PAPER COMPANY
Hemp, handmade paintable papers, and recycled wrapping paper
www.greenfieldpaper.com

OF THE EARTH
Tree-free decorative paper
www.custompaper.com

RAWGANIQUE
Hemp paper sketchbooks
www.rawganique.com

RECYCLED AND HANDMADE PAPERS
www.handmade-paper.us

RHIMAX ORGANIC PAPER
www.rhimax.net

CANVAS AND SUSTAINABLE STRETCHER BARS

BLANK CANVAS CO.
Canvas and Sustainable stretcher bars
www.blankcanvasco.com

EARTH FRIENDLY GOODS
Hemp canvas
www.earthfriendlygoods.com

HEMPTRADERS
Hemp canvas
www.hemptraders.com

JOHN JONES
Sustainable wood stretcher bars
www.johnjones.co.uk

NEARSEA NATURALS
Hemp and organic cotton canvas
www.nearseanaturals.com

PEGASUS ART SHOP
Sustainable wood stretcher bars
www.pegasusart.co.uk

PERMA JET
Sustainable stretcher bars
www.permajet.com

STRETCHED CANVAS LTD.
Canvas and sustainable stretcher bars
www.stretched-canvas.com

MISCELLANEOUS ART SUPPLIES

AMERICAN SCIENCE AND SURPLUS
Offers an interesting selection of closeouts, inventory overruns, mis-manufactures, and items whose time has not come
www.sciplus.com

ARTSUPPLY.COM
Eco-friendly art supplies
www.artsupply.com

BUDGET ART MATERIALS
Eco-friendly art supplies
www.budgetartmaterials.com

ECO ART WORKS
Eco-friendly art supplies
www.ecoartworks.com

FINE ART STORE
Recycled canvas boards
www.fineartstore.com

OBJECTS AND ELEMENTS
Nontoxic resins and repurposed jewelry supplies
www.objectsandelements.com

PRANG SOYBEAN CRAYONS
www.dixonusa.com

RACINES OFFICE AND ART SUPPLIES
Eco-friendly art supplies
www.racinesfortbragg.com

TASKBOARD
Made from sustainable forestry wood
www.taskboard.com

RECYCLE CENTERS FOR ALTERNATIVE ART MATERIALS

ART FROM SCRAP
Santa Barbara, California
www.artfromscrap.org

ARTS AND SCRAPS
Detroit, Michigan
www.artsandscraps.org

EAST BAY DEPOT FOR CREATIVE REUSE
Oakland, California
www.ciwmb.ca.gov/reuse/profiles/eastbay.htm

HUDSON VALLEY MATERIALS EXCHANGE
New Paltz, New York
www.hvme.com

MATERIALS FOR THE ARTS
Long Island City, New York
www.mfta.org

MATERIALS RESOURCE CENTER
Ronkonkoma, New York
www.craftmaterialsresource.com

RECYCLED MATERIALS CENTER
Children's Museum of Kansas
www.kidmuzm.org

RECYCLE SHOP
Boston Children's Museum, Massachusetts
www.bostonchildrensmuseum.org/exhibits/recycle.html

RESOURCE DEPOT
Riviera Beach, Florida
www.resourcedepot.net

THE SCRAP BOX
Ann Arbor, Michigan
www.scrapbox.org

THE SCRAP EXCHANGE
Durham, North Carolina
www.scrapexchange.org

SCRAP—THE SCHOOL AND COMMUNITY REUSE ACTION PROJECT
Portland, Oregon
www.scrapaction.org

SCRAP—SCROUNGERS' CENTER FOR REUSABLE ART PARTS
San Francisco, California
www.scrap-sf.org

ST. LOUIS TEACHERS' RECYCLE CENTER
St. Louis, Missouri
www.stlouisteachersrecycle.homestead.com

URBAN SOURCE
Vancouver, British Columbia
www.urbansource.bc.ca

ONLINE RESOURCES

ART AND MATERIALS INSTITUTE, INC. (ACMI)
www.acminet.org

CALIFORNIA'S PROPOSITION 65
www.oehha.org/prop65.html

EARTH 911
A searchable database for finding recycling and reuse locations
www.earth911.org

EARTH DAY NETWORK
Raising environmental awareness around the world
www.earthdaynetwork.org

ECO STREET
An online journal of all things green
www.ecostreet.com

ELEVATE YOUR STANDARDS
Ecological guide to paper
www.celerydesign.com/paper/matrix.html

EVE'S GARDEN ECOLOGY RESOURCE CENTER
www.evesgarden.org

GOLDEN ARTIST COLORS ENVIRONMENTAL GUIDELINES
www.goldenpaints.com/healthsafety/environ/index.php

GOLDEN ARTIST COLORS HEALTH AND SAFETY GUIDELINES
www.goldenpaints.com/healthsafety/health/index.php

Golden Artist Colors: Removing Water-based Paint Solids from Rinse Water Article
www.goldenpaints.com/justpaint/jp3article3.php

Green Arts Web
Information and resources on environmental art
www.greenarts.org

Health and Safety in the Arts
A searchable database of health and safety information for artists including pigments and mediums
www.tucsonaz.gov/arthazards

Hemphasis
Everything you want to know about hemp
www.hemphasis.net

Liquitex Safe Studio Tips
www.liquitex.com/healthsafety/safestudiotips
.cfm

Living in Paper
Building with recycled paper
www.livinginpaper.com

National Geographic Green Guide
Green living tips, product reviews, environmental health news
www.thegreenguide.com

Natural Pigments: Educational Resources for Artists
www.naturalpigments.com/education

Vermont Safety Information Resources, Inc.
Material Safety Data information
www.hazard.com/msds/index.php

ARTIST RESOURCES AND ORGANIZATIONS

Artists in Nature International Network
Resources for artists and communities interested in nature
www.artinnature.org

Centre for Contemporary Art and the Natural World
United Kingdom
www.ccanw.co.uk

Coalition of Green Artists
http://greenartists.tripod.com

Eco-Art at Teaneck Creek Conservancy
New Jersey eco-art programs
www.teaneckcreek.org

Eco Art Network
www.ecoartnetwork.org

Ecoartspace
Resources for environmental artists and organizations
www.ecoartspace.org

Dreamfish
A network of creative change-makers
www.dreamfish.com

Future Sea Level
Raising awareness about rising sea levels through art
www.futuresealevel.org

Green Art
France
www.greenart.info

Islands Institute of Interdisciplinary Studies
Canada
www.islandsinstitute.com

Maho Bay Trash to Treasures Art Center
St. John, U.S. Virgin Islands
www.maho.org

San Francisco Recycling and Disposal Artist in Residence Program
www.sfrecycling.com/air

Pow Wow Eco-Arts
United Kingdom
www.powwow-ecoarts.org.uk

Royal Society for the Arts (RSA)
United Kingdom
www.thersa.org.uk

Social Land Art Project
Germany
www.slap.de

WEAD: Women Environmental Artists Directory
www.weadartists.org

GREEN GALLERIES AND STUDIOS

Boom Museum
Virtual interactive museum for art, the Netherlands
www.boommuseum.nl

Eco-Logical Art
Los Angeles, California
www.eco-logicalart.org

EnvironmentalArt.net
Environmental art from Finland
www.environmentalart.net

Green Museum
An online environmental-art museum
www.greenmuseum.org

Halikonlahti Green Art
Finland
www.halikonlahti.net

KOZO Studio and Gallery
Ireland
www.kozogallery.com

Natural World Museum
A global cultural institution
www.artintoaction.org

Thoreau Center for Sustainability
San Francisco, California
New York, New York
www.thoreau.org

Sitka Center for Art and Ecology
Otis, Oregon
www.sitkacenter.org

TEMPLATES

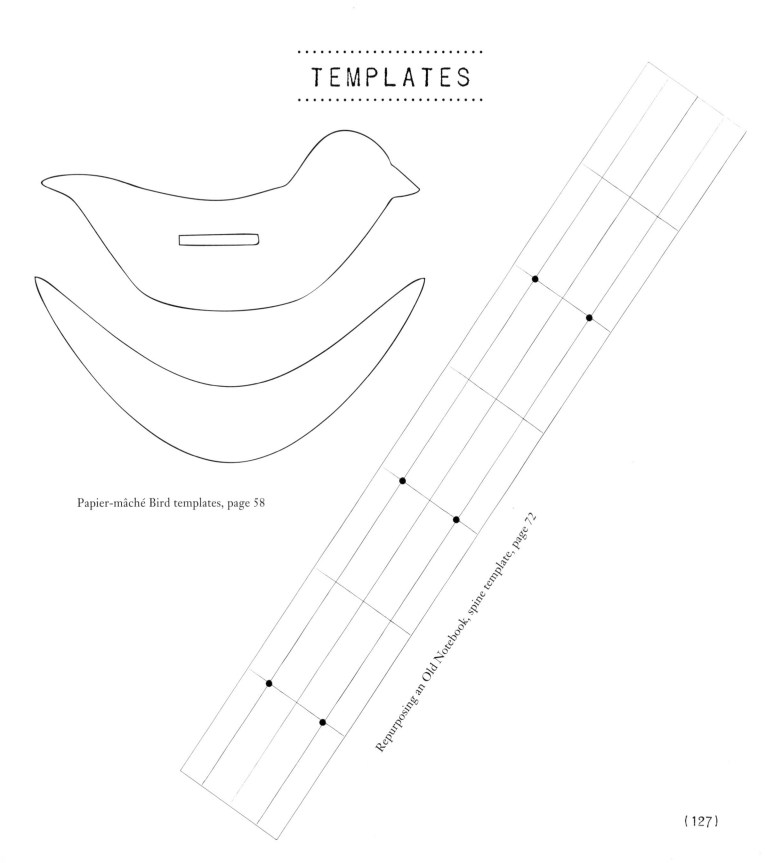

Papier-mâché Bird templates, page 58

Repurposing an Old Notebook, spine template, page 72

ABOUT THE AUTHORS

KAREN MICHEL

Karen Michel is a mixed-media artist and lives in New York, where she runs a nonprofit art center for kids, the Creative Art Space for Kids Foundation, with her artist husband, Carlo Thertus. Along with sharing her love for the arts with children, she also teaches adult workshops throughout the United States, Canada, and Mexico. Her books, paintings, and collages have been exhibited internationally and have been published in various books and magazines. She is the author of *The Complete Guide to Altered Imagery: Mixed-Media Techniques for Collage, Altered Books, Artist Journals, and More* (Quarry Books). To view more of her work, visit www.karenmichel.com

ACKNOWLEDGMENTS

I would like to thank the contributing artists for generously sharing their vision of green, Kristen Hampshire for the hard work and time she put into the contributing artist interviews, and the team at Quarry Books for helping me reign in this wild creature of a book and make it a reality.

KRISTEN HAMPSHIRE

Kristen Hampshire is an award-winning writer and author of four outdoor design and landscaping books, including *John Deere's Lawn Care & Landscaping*; *52 Backyard Projects: Design, Build and Plant the Yard of Your Dreams One Weekend at a Time*; *Hobby Farms*; and *Stonescaping Made Simple*. Hampshire has been published in more than 30 periodicals including *Ladies' Home Journal*, *Fortune Small Business*, *Vogue Knitting*, *The Tennessean*, *Ohio* magazine, and *Consumers Digest*.

She works from her bungalow in Bay Village, Ohio, where she lives with her husband Haven Ohly and Miss Mayzie, her Scottish Terrier and muse. Visit Hampshire online at www.kristenhampshire.com.